MW01227600

POWERFUL
GOOD NEWS

POWERFUL

GOOD

NEWS

The Heartwarming Message
of the New Testament Gospel

Robert J. Wieland

CFI Book Division
Gordonsville, Tennessee

Copyright © 2019 by CFI Book Division

Cover and interior design by CFI Graphic Design

All Rights Reserved. No part of this book may be reproduced in any form or by any electronic or mechanical means including information storage and retrieval systems without permission from its publisher, CFI Book Division.

Bible quotations in this book are from the following versions:

Unless otherwise noted Bible quotations are from *The New King James Version*, Copyright © 1979, 1980, 1982 by Thomas Nelson, Inc.

(KJV) King James Version, Copyright ©1988, B. B. Kirkebride Bible Company, Inc., Indianapolis, IN.

(GNB) *Good News Bible, Today's English Version*, American Bible Society, New York, NY, 1976.

(NIV) *New International Version*, Zondervan Publishing House, Grand Rapids, MI, 1986.

(NEB) *The New English Bible*, Oxford University Press, New York, NY, 1971.

(Phillips) *The New Testament in Modern English*, Geoffrey Bles, London, © J. B. Phillips, 1960.

Published by CFI Book Division

P.O. Box 159, Gordonsville, Tennessee 38563

ISBN-10: 0-9975122-6-1
ISBN-13: 978-0-9975122-6-7

Printed in the United States of America

Typeset in 11.5/13.8 Minion Pro

The title of this book reflects the Greek word *dunamis* that in the New Testament is translated "power." The same word is the root for the English word dynamite. Rightly understood, the Gospel's message is *dynamite* to all who believe its powerful Good News to transform human lives.

Contents

Introduction

In my fifty years of pastoral ministry counseling people with spiritual problems, I think I can safely say that never have I met someone discouraged or defeated spiritually whose problem did not come from one or the other of two causes: either he or she had never understood how good the Good News of the gospel is, or had never truly believed it.

If you read the simple record of Jesus' sayings in the four Gospels, you will find over and over that He has good news for sincere people who long for peace. He said, "The Lord has anointed Me to preach good tidings to the poor; He has sent Me to heal the brokenhearted, to proclaim liberty to the captives, and the opening of the prison to those who are bound" (Isaiah 61:1).

This book is based on the premise that such Good News packs a powerful punch. The power is not in the personality of the messenger, but in the message itself. Especially is this evident in the New Testament truth of justification by faith.

For many people, that doctrine is a dry-as-dust bore; my prayer is that this modest attempt to make it live will set your heart singing for now and for eternity.

—Robert J. Wieland

CHAPTER ONE

God's Arms Around the World

In the debris of the ruin of ancient empires we find a priceless gem of indescribable beauty—the New Testament Good News. It once saved civilization from suicide.

Most of the problem that plagues the world centers in the inherent evil of human nature. Somehow it manipulates society and individuals to choose the selfish way. Hence the horrors we face such as the drug culture, corruption, crime, war—a threatening of global ruin.

Admittedly, light is stronger than darkness, but is it also true that good is stronger than evil? Can love possibly triumph over hatred? (For example, can the Middle East ever learn to love? Can cocaine billionaires be converted?) Can good news overcome bad news?

Millions of troubled youth doubt it. They have a gut feeling that humanity's fate is doomed. If AIDS doesn't kill us off, depleting the ozone layer will. "Tomorrow we die," they say, and they give themselves to hedonistic indulgence today.

Their cynicism is at least rational. They know the world's resources could wipe out hunger and want, yet massive poverty mocks us. They sense that if other people's problems are incurable, someday their own will be the same. The 17th century John Donne exposes our true feelings which are perhaps unconscious but nonetheless significant:

"If a clod be washed away by the sea, Europe is the less, … any man's death diminishes me, because I am involved in mankind, and therefore never send to know for whom the bell tolls; it tolls for thee." [1]

Not only are the youth troubled. Grandparents worry about what kind of a life they will bequeath to their grandchildren. As long as

---

1. John Donne, Meditation #17 from *Devotions Upon Emergent Occasions* XVII (1624).

hunger and futility overwhelm the masses in the Third World (which now includes America's inner cities), security in our own world must become increasingly fragile. Can we remain forever a fortress of peaceful plenty in an ocean of resentful want? Must our grandchildren barricade their homes behind AK-47s?

In our own North America we face a disturbing disintegration of society. In 1964 President Lyndon Johnson promised that the "days of the dole are numbered." More than five decades and hundreds of billions of dollars later, where is the "Great Society"?[2] The poor generally are poorer and the rich are richer.

While our poor are getting desperate, the well-to-do also find that the problems of coping take a lethal toll on the human psyche. Richard Reeves, writing for the Universal Press Syndicate, says that "a lot of us crack—defeated by drugs or alcohol, envy or mobility, our own devils or weakness. … Is America going crazy?"

If America with all its money and think-tank capabilities can't solve its problems of drugs, crime, illiteracy, violence, and poverty, youth wonder what hope there is for the world itself. America's freedom example has been "the last, best hope of mankind." If this nation destroys itself, new Hitlers and Idi Amins will start blossoming everywhere.

Insight magazine says that our crime-infested poverty has "assumed horrific dimensions in the cities." The progressive decay of the inner cities shocks those who remember only a few years back an era of civility and security. Vans in Harlem now pull up to the sidewalk to sell crack to a line of people twenty deep. "My worst dreams, my worst, were nowhere near this," says Shakoor Aljuwani of the Youth Action Construction Training Program. "I never thought it could ever have gotten this bad."

Why, with their eyes wide open, do human beings walk right into cocaine and other addictions? Something is dreadfully wrong, because these addictions are fundamentally suicide. Only a *very* sick species will destroy itself. Unless change comes soon, a conceivable scenario for the 21st century may be a polarized society—hideously

---

2. Time references have been updated in this new edition to reflect the 30 years that have elapsed since the last publication date.

massive prisons and hospitals for criminals, AIDS victims, and drug zombies, with "normal" people slaving full time to support them.

An ominous cloud on the not-too-distant horizon suggests the possible coming of a "born-again" Hitler who will yield to outraged public pressure and arrange a cheaper "final solution," this time for criminals, junkies, and miscellaneous undesirables. Nazism was the surfacing of a subterranean stream of collective dementia, perennially waiting for a crisis of popular wrath.

Some sober non-religious analysts now openly blame adolescent sex and marital infidelity as the root cause of our exploding poverty-crime-addiction syndrome. While solid marriages almost always lead to reasonable prosperity and order, single-parent families, with some exceptions, tend to gravitate toward deeper want.

Is It Hard to Believe in a God of Love?

Daniel Moynihan[3] says broken families "ask for and get chaos. Crime, violence, unrest, disorder ... are very near to inevitable." Television and movies propagate raw infidelity of every kind. It's the moral ferment that Jesus predicted for our days: "Because iniquity shall abound, the love of many shall wax cold" (Matthew 24:12, KJV). It waxes cold because people no longer believe in it.

"Iniquity" is lawlessness, an inner heart-rebellion against God's moral principles. If we find it hard to conceive of the existence of a righteous God, all we need to do is to start reasoning backward from the reality of evil: "The carnal mind is enmity against God; for it is not subject to the law of God" (Romans 8:7). The mystery of perverse human nature is sufficient to prove that the Bible is true because the reality of evil presupposes the existence of good, just as a shadow presupposes a light behind the obstruction.

Whether a person is religious or not, he or she can hardly deny that we have come to a time precisely delineated by Jesus when He said that "men's hearts [will be] failing them from fear and the expectation

---

3. Daniel Patrick Moynihan (1927-2003) was an American politician, sociologist, and diplomat. A member of the Democratic Party, he represented New York in the United States Senate, and served as an adviser to Republican U.S. President Richard Nixon.

of those things which are coming on the earth" (Luke 21:26). The better informed one is, the more he is haunted by the shadows of tomorrow.

But there is hope. As the daily news gets worse, there is Good News that gets better.

Our Dark Future Is Lighted

The Bible comes on stage with a breath-taking message of hope. It assures us there is a personal God, a Heavenly Father, a Creator-Savior, who actually loves this "crazy," cruel, selfish, violent, immoral, devilish world.

This Good News outweighs all the bad news because He is the source of a love that is positive, active, and by its nature has to be effective.

The best-known words in many languages are these: "God so loved the world that He gave His only begotten Son, that whoever believes in Him should not perish but have everlasting life" (John 3:16). Most of us find it hard to hug a filthy, repulsive human being. God is hugging this planet to His heart, bad and dirty as it is. He is like a father embracing a prodigal son, taking the evil into Himself and purging it. This love is the most stupendous truth that mankind can contemplate.

This new idea astonished the sophisticated world of New Testament times. Probably as great a percentage of population then as now believed in a Supreme Being, but both Roman aristocrats and slaves found it incomprehensible that God actually cared for worthless humanity. If He did, how could He watch such injustices as slavery, political corruption, and the gladiatorial bloodshed in the Coliseum, and not *do* something?

Imagine the stir raised by the apostles when they insisted that God actually *loves* mean, selfish, cruel, bad people. Not that He loves their badness, but He loves *them*. "He loves slaves, gladiators, prostitutes, murderers, rapacious tax-collectors, cruel emperors?" asked the Romans. "Yes," said the apostles. "God did not send His Son into the world to condemn the world; but that the world through Him might be saved" (verse 17). This was a radical, revolutionary idea for people who had looked upon God as indifferently patronizing to good people and hateful to the evil ones.

But such an overturning of ancient values could never convince people unless solid evidence backed it up. The apostles must prove that they did not invent such a love from their own imagination. Evidence there was, and it was incontestable: when the Son of God was executed by cruel Roman soldiers, He did the unthinkable—He loved and prayed for His enemies, "Father, forgive them, for they do not know what they do" (Luke 23:34).

No one could remember that anyone had ever before said anything like that. For all the world to see, Christ had demonstrated that "God is love" (1 John 4:8), a genuine kind that humanity could not fake. Now the world was on its way to being turned upside down (Acts 17:6).

No creature from Mars could have aroused more astonishment than this new idea. A love that depends neither on the beauty of its object nor on its goodness? A love that not only loves ugly and mean people without value, but that actually creates value in them? When people heard about this, they demanded to know more.

The best thinkers of that day had praised the love of the Greek Alcestis for Admetus as the supreme revelation of divine goodness—she was willing to die for a *good* man. The apostles said no, that's not the real thing: "The proof of God's amazing love is this: that it was *while we were sinners* that Christ died for us. ... while we were His enemies" (Romans 5:8, 10, Phillips). Jews and Romans looked at one another in amazement.

If there was a God, the ancients imagined Him residing in lofty isolation, waiting for humans to seek Him out. Christ revealed Him in stark contrast as a personal Savior "come to seek and to save that which was lost" (Luke 19:10).

The Practical Effect of This New Idea of Love

People who heard that News became delirious with joy. Now their humdrum existence suddenly took on precious meaning. Sorrow, disappointment, pain, even the endurance of slavery, and yes, martyrdom, became honored and sacred in the light of such a new revelation. Death lost its terror because Christ had robbed it of its sting (1 Corinthians 15:55-57). God Himself has come close to us, they said, taking upon Himself our nature, suffering with us, corporately becoming one with us! Every believing slave became a prince and every believing prince was ready to kneel down beside his slave.

There was no end to the ramifications of this astounding idea. By coming in the person of His Son, to seek that which was lost, God had done something that seemed incomprehensible. He had stepped down lower and lower into such dark levels of condescension that He reached a depth beyond which humiliation itself could not exist.

Those who heard the apostles saw a stairway, not leading from man up to God but steps He took in descending to the lowest level of our fallen humanity. Not only did He leave the angels behind and humble Himself in becoming a man, He was born in a filthy hovel where rude animals seek shelter. Then He lived a peasant life of menial service and hard work. At its end He chose to be obedient unto ultimate death, facing its horror head-on instead of trying to evade judgment as does the suicide.

And that was not all. What got people's minds swirling was the story that when this Son of God had been rejected by the leaders of His own people, they crucified Him as a criminal on a Roman cross. This meant, as everyone understood, that He endured the ultimate emotional distress of being rejected by God, for it was anciently believed that "he who is hanged [on a tree] is accursed of God" (Deuteronomy 21:23; Galatians 3:13). (We will discuss this in chapter 6.)

The Son of God had suffered the equivalent of hell! He had sacrificed not only His life here and now, but His hopes for eternity. That kept men up all night thinking and talking about it. They grappled with the effort to "comprehend with all the saints what is the width and length and depth and height—to know the love of Christ which passes knowledge" (Ephesians 3:18, 19). He could not see His resurrection coming up.

In the process of contemplating this divine deed, a phenomenal life-changing power was unleashed. After forgetting your meals while you searched out this truth, you found yourself facing life as a new person. A different purpose for living now transcended pain or pleasure. Such love accomplished the impossible for high and low, rich and poor, free and slave: it released "those who through fear of death were all their lifetime subject to bondage" (Hebrews 2:15). The common denominator lying beneath pain in all human sorrow had evaporated. Catch the thrill those people felt:

> In this the love of God was manifested toward us, that God has sent His only begotten Son into the world, that we might live through Him. ... Love [*agape*] has been among us in this: that we may have boldness in the day of judgment;

because as He is, so are we in this world. There is no fear in love; but perfect love casts out fear (1 John 4:9-18).

Christ's Resurrection Proved the Gospel True

And then to cap off the glorious Good News, this Son of God had risen from the dead on the third day after His ignominious execution. He had declared in triumph that He possessed the keys of death and the grave, so that all whose hearts appreciated the dimensions of His revolutionary love would triumph over death with Him (Revelation 1:17, 18).

The life-changing dynamics of this love are encapsulated in a priceless gem from Paul. He tells why and how those who believed this love found power in its Good News:

The love of Christ constraineth [motivates] us; because we thus judge, that if One died for all, then were all dead: and that He died for all, that they which live should not henceforth live unto themselves, but unto Him which died for them, and rose again (2 Corinthians 5:14, 15, KJV).

At last a divine truth had penetrated the inmost defenses of our egocentric mindset. Like a heat-seeking missile it had sought the source of our me-first selfishness and annihilated it. Thus the root whence sprang all the bitter fruit of human evil had been eradicated by this humble sacrifice and glorious resurrection of Christ. Almost overnight believing human beings who had been mean, ugly, and cruel were transformed into loving, lovable people. And those on top of the heap who thought they had all that heart could wish discovered how empty worldly success is without Christ. The Good News had done it.

A New Testament document written by Paul supplies a partial list of the various categories of addiction-deliverance which this simple gospel accomplished. Believers had been former "fornicators," "idolaters," "adulterers," "homosexuals," "sodomites," "thieves," "covetous" (what we would call "shopaholics"), alcoholics, and embezzlers. "Such were some of you," says the apostle to the Corinthian congregation. But they experienced deliverance from those ingrown obsessions and became "washed" and "sanctified," new people (see 1 Corinthians 6:9-11).

There was nothing these people did to *achieve* such exhilarating freedom from their psychic chains; they had *seen* something and *believed* it—the Good News of the atonement of the Son of God. In a world where selfish cruelty was as common as dirt, this revelation was a catharsis. In the previous thousands of years of history, no philosopher, playwright, poet, or priest, had ever imagined such astonishing ideas.

The Same Good News Is Powerful Today

That love of God for sinners is still the best Good News anyone will ever hear. It is positive, active, persistent, seeking, and therefore just as powerful today as it has ever been. No way can anyone ignore it. Either you believe it or you disbelieve it. No one can sit on the fence after hearing it truthfully proclaimed.

The most horrible evils our modern world knows stem from that same source of human selfishness as cursed the world of the apostles' day. Could that same Good News transform the cocaine merchants and their addicts, the prostitutes, the embezzlers, the racists, the murderers, the sensual materialists, of today? Millions of people say Yes. Even more important, the Holy Spirit through the Bible says Yes. It also transforms the wealthy and educated, the self-sufficient, hard-hearted tycoons, scientists, and politicians.

Three presuppositions make the truth of this unique love *appear* difficult to believe: (1) Since self-respecting people don't hug dirty, undeserving bad people, why should God do so? (2) How can an infinite God have feelings like we humans have? (3) If He really loves the world, why doesn't He prove it by *doing* something to halt its present slide to ruin?

Many assume that answers are impossible. Conventional wisdom indeed has none, but here is where the Bible takes the spotlight and refutes the doubts head-on.

We will consider these questions in the next chapter

CHAPTER TWO

Why Doesn't God
Do Something?

While it is true that we humans don't love dirty, undeserving, bad people, the Bible says that God *does* love them. This is because of the unique quality of His love (John 3:16). Whereas human love is dependent on the beauty or goodness of its object, God's love is sovereign and independent. That's why it is free to love evil people. He loved them in Christ, and He still has His arms flung around this world (2 Corinthians 5:19-21). He is still the Good Shepherd seeking His lost sheep (Luke 15:3-7), corporately involved with humanity so that our suffering has become His suffering (see 1 Corinthians 12:12, 26, 27). The human race is one in Christ, so that He is now part of our family. He cannot forget or forsake His own family!

> This is my Father's world;
>   O let me ne'er forget
>   That though the wrong seems oft so strong,
>   God is the Ruler yet.

> This is my Father's world;
>   Why should my heart be sad?
>   The Lord is King; let the heavens ring!
>   God reigns; let earth be glad![1]

Our problem lies in distinguishing between what we call love and the nature of the love that the Bible reveals. When it says that "God is love," the word in Greek is *agape*, a foreign concept imported from heaven, something wholly absent from native earth-consciousness

---

1. Maltbie D. Babcock, "This Is My Father's World," 1901.

anywhere. No ancient religion outside the Old Testament had the resources even to hint of its existence.

However scientific our mind may be today, however logical and rational in its attempts to doubt the personality of God, the reality of *agape* confronts us squarely. We can deny it like a blind man may deny sunlight, but if we are honest, it testifies to us of a loving, personal God who is both Father and Savior of the world. This love blocks agnosticism or atheism in its tracks until such time as conscience either acknowledges it or succumbs to cynical unbelief. Beyond that rejection, even God's angels can do no more.

No historian, evolutionist, or atheist can trace the origin of *agape* to any other source than that of a cross erected on a little hill outside Jerusalem. If the fishermen-apostles had minds fertile enough to invent *that* idea, they would deserve the all-time Pulitzer Prize.

How Can an Infinite God Have Feelings Like We Have?

An airliner with hundreds of innocent passengers blown out of the sky, a demented murderer spraying machine gun bullets on a school yard of innocent children, an earthquake killing thousands of sleeping people—how can an almighty God in heaven look on such things and allow them if He loves and if He has feelings? Millions of people want to believe in Him, but wonder if He is an impassive Buddha-like deity, an absentee Landlord who ignores His tenants on Planet Earth.

If the Bible is right when it says that God is a divine Person, it is easy to assume that He must be ensconced in perfect security, immortal, enjoying constant pleasure with millions of angels serving Him. From our viewpoint, the residents of a Beverly Hills mansion needn't worry about homeless beggars in Calcutta.

Deism is the widely popular assumption that although God exists, He is coldly distant, leaving us to our inept selves. Because such an idea breeds selfishness, it is very bad news. If Number One is a devotee of number one, why shouldn't we be the same? The assumption that God is as selfish or unconcerned as we are is the real reason why "me-first" has become such a popular philosophy. All the world's selfishness derives either from a false concept of God or a blatant rejection of its truth.

The Bible picture of God's true character reveals Him as a Person, with a human side. He does care, He does feel earth's hurt, He is concerned. He has sensitive and sympathetic feelings, which means He is in deep pain.

In fact, He cannot rest so long as there is one unhappy person left on the earth. His heartache is incessant for He is infinitely close to humanity.

For example, His involvement in the minute nuances of our heart-longings is down-to-earth: "For only a penny you can buy two sparrows, yet not one sparrow falls to the ground without your Father's consent" (Matthew 10:29, GNB). He is so corporately involved in our experiences that He has nerve-endings that sense our pain as fully as we feel it, yes even more so, for at no time is our consciousness alert to the full dimensions of pain's potential. The teenager getting hooked on drugs or immorality cannot foresee the agony in his or her future; God sees and feels all of it ahead of time. (If only the teenager could!)

Speaking of God's suffering followers on earth, Isaiah says: "In all their affliction He was afflicted. He ... bore them and carried them all the days of old" (Isaiah 63:9).

Christ's name is "'Immanuel,' which is translated, 'God with us'" (Matthew 1:23). In other words, there can be no hurt that a human knows that He does not also feel. Isaiah further explicates this divine consciousness: "Surely He has borne our griefs and carried our sorrows. ... He was wounded for our transgressions, He was bruised for our iniquities; the chastisement of our peace was upon Him" (Isaiah 53:4, 5). Our otherwise intolerable existence can be transformed by simply believing that often-unbelieved glimpse of God as a sensitive, loving Person.

Even in the midst of our troubles, we humans still enjoy a vast amount of peace, though we may not be conscious of its true source. What Isaiah is saying is this: None of us could know the "credit" benefit of even a moment of fleeting happiness unless a corresponding "debit" had been already borne in our stead by that divine Suffering One. This is the underlying truth behind every human joy, every springtime, every delicious strawberry.

He was rejected on earth and expelled, for the people said, "We will not have this Man to reign over us" (Luke 19:14). Instead of the bitter rejection which He felt, we experience His unconditional acceptance of us, which includes the Father's also. It's amazing, not only that He has forgiven His murderers, but that He has not in high dudgeon washed His hands of our predicament. We may richly deserve to be without Him, but in the fullest sense possible He assures us, "Lo, I am with you always, even to the end of the world" (Matthew 28:20).

Jesus' work was to reveal the facts about His Father's character. Not only are Christ and the Father one, but since Christ has become incorporate in humanity and we in Him, our yearnings and life experiences become His. This staggers our imagination, for we find it hard to believe that Good News can be that good.

But it is.

But our question is: If God is so concerned about us, and if He is all-powerful, and if He feels our suffering, how can He allow evil to go on?

Is He Doing All He Can?

The Bible discloses a behind-the-scenes cosmic conflict. There is a very good reason for what superficially *appears* to be unconcern on His part. The truth is, He is very much concerned. But He has an enemy who is fighting a war against Him. This explains what appears to be a mysterious impotence on the part of God.

We are not surprised at rebellions and wars on earth, but who would expect such to happen in heaven? That's where evil started:

> War broke out in heaven: Michael[2] and His angels fought against the dragon; and the dragon and his angels fought, but they did not prevail, nor was a place found for them in heaven any longer. So the great dragon was cast out, that serpent of old, called the Devil and Satan, who deceives the whole world; he was cast to the earth, and his angels were cast out with him. ... "Woe to the inhabitants of the earth and the sea! For the devil has come down to you, having great wrath, because he knows that he has a short time" (Revelation 12:7-12).

During World War II, the subjects of the British crown endured years of agony, while a kind and sensitive King George VI and his gracious queen sat on the throne. The king listened to the daily news of destruction, his own heart torn with sympathy for the agony of his subjects. Gladly would he have ended the war at any moment if he could. But the war was not of his making. Adolf Hitler had thrust the conflict upon him, and the security of Europe required that it be fought through to the bitter end.

---

2. Another name for Christ; see John 5:26-29; Jude 9; 1 Thessalonians 4:16.

This is a miniscule glimpse of the problem that God has. An enemy has thrust this greater war upon Him—a controversy not of His choosing. The cosmic drama of the conflict between good and evil began with Act I—the war in heaven where Satan met defeat. Act II is of our making, introducing the insurrection into this planet. Our first parents, Adam and Eve, signed this world over to the control of God's enemy and made themselves his captives. Here the rebel managed to recoup his loss in Act I.

God's love could not abandon the world. The very nature of that love required Him to rescue us. Thus, Act III. The Father must endure intimate sympathy with the agony on this planet until the great conflict between Christ and Satan can be resolved.

Christ came two thousand years ago to claim His rightful place as the world's Ruler. If He had been accepted, we would long ago have realized the world peace, security, and happiness that we yearn for. But since He was rejected, crucified, cast out of His world, the planet itself is still in rebellion against Him, and no more recognizes His authority than did the Nazis that of George VI or Franklin Roosevelt. While there are people today who wholeheartedly accept Christ as the rightful Ruler of this planet, they are in the minority, fighting "underground" as it were.

The Lord is eager to return to this earth to end this nightmare of selfishness and sin with all its attendant cruelty. No way is He sitting by idly, enjoying Himself in celestial luxury while the war rages on. His love for the world is intense. The universe itself can hardly wait for the cosmic V-Day when the cruel enemy shall be forever defeated (Romans 8:19-23).

One of the most profound disclosures of Scripture is that one of our days is to God like a thousand years (2 Peter 3:8). To us the darkest day is always short, for the pain we can feel is finite, only our own or at best a partial sympathy felt for those few nearest us. But in deep sensitivity God must feel the pain of everyone on earth. Surely that must make one of our collective days seem like a thousand years to Him. He has so much more consciousness pressed into a day than we have. Imagine sharing in the agony of millions, yes billions, of people! He can never go to sleep as we can (Psalm 121:3). He longs ever so much for this planet's pain to come to an end.

His solution to world problems is infinitely efficient: no band-aids to apply in spectacular but futile experiments. He must get to the root of human problems—the sinful selfishness entrenched in human hearts. All the suffering in the world is in some way its consequence. In order to solve the problem, that source of evil must be eradicated. Not that selfish people must be eradicated, but selfishness itself must be. This must be accomplished by proclaiming and demonstrating the Good News of what Christ accomplished on His cross and what He continues to do as the world's High Priest, as Savior from that sin.

Satan opposes this. His last-ditch stand is his claim that the sacrifice of Christ and His on-going ministry in heaven are an exercise in futility. Look, he sneers, the world is worse now than it was when the Son of God died for its salvation!

To answer this charge, the gospel must produce a beautiful change in believing humanity, and thus give evidence that the plan of salvation is not in vain. Enter Act IV.

Is there such a gospel? Is it *really* Good News? Does it have power? If so, how does it work? The precious message the Lord sends to the world is not a thunder-and-lightning denunciation of sin abounding, but a heart-warming message of *much more* abounding *grace*. That is what penetrates to the inner badness of human evil and changes hearts.

God's Present Problem

When you and I pray, "Please, Lord, why don't You *do* something to help this sad world?" the answer comes back to us, "Why don't *you* do something?" By His rejection and crucifixion, Christ has been voted out of office on this planet. He cannot stage a coup and usurp control where He is not wanted, but He can work in and through those people who commit themselves to Him and who respond to His Holy Spirit.

He is "the true Light which gives light to every man who comes into the world" (John 1:9). Not all welcome and receive the light, but some do, thank God. He has encircled the world with an atmosphere of grace as real as the air we breathe. Those who choose to welcome it become His children and His co-workers.

He will have the cooperation of the "underground" forces who are loyal to Him in this great controversy, ministering that grace in a practical way to the world. The only hands He can use, the only voice through which He can speak, are ours.

The rebel unfortunately also has collaborators: Christians who deny the gospel. As the true gospel propagates light, so its denial actually propagates darkness. The darkness-gospel looks good in that it regales us with good advice, detailed instruction about *what* to do. The problem is that we don't know *how* to do what is right. What we need to know is what *Christ* has done and is doing. Only that knowledge will make it possible for us to be transformed.

But people who think they believe Christ's gospel can be obsessed with a subtle, camouflaged legalism. It's the idea that "we-must-do-this," "we-must-do-that," "we-must-work-more," "we-must-be-more-faithful," "we-must-get-the-victory," "we-must-study-more," "we-must-pray-more," "we-must-witness-more," *ad infinitum*. Always the idea is that we have to work at this or that; a debt hangs over us, an obligation that crushes us. The root poison of self-concern remains in spite of all these human efforts. Ross D. London, writing in *Newsweek*, April 24, 1989, says that "if one chooses good only to gain heaven and avoid hell, one simply acts out of self-interest." This is the essence of legalism.

Many join the Jews of Christ's day in asking, "What shall we *do* that we might work the works of God?" They don't listen to that divine answer that Jesus gave, perhaps with a sigh, "This is the work of God, that ye *believe*. ... " (John 6:28, 29). There is a latent fear of the power of such true faith lest we end up not doing enough good works. It has been assumed for centuries that the only motivation that will be effective is the fear of eternal damnation if one does not do everything just right.

But a distorted "gospel" based on fear can produce only frustration, discouragement, and spiritual impotence. And widespread *laissez-faire* in almost every religion testifies to that prevailing distortion. The problem is that faith is not understood as a heart-appreciation of the heavenly love that casts out fear (1 John 4:17-19).

A Better Motivation Is the Answer

The pure, true gospel reveals a *faith which works*. That is why "it is the power of God to salvation" (Romans 1:16). It produces heart-acceptance of, and obedience to, all the truth. The inspired apostle "determined not to know anything among you except Jesus Christ and Him crucified. ... My speech and my preaching were not with persuasive words of human wisdom, but in demonstration of the Spirit and of power" (1 Corinthians 2:2, 4). In these last days the Lord has promised that again such a message will be proclaimed worldwide, a message that transcends fear and truly casts it out.

25

The reason why it works is that it replaces legalistic imperatives with gospel enablings: "I saw another angel flying in the midst of heaven, having *the everlasting gospel* to preach to … every nation, tribe, tongue, and people." This angel calls upon us to "fear God," that is, to appreciate His character, "and give glory to Him, for the hour of His judgment has come" (Revelation 14:6, 7, emphasis added). The idea is to honor Him, to appreciate the honest reality of His character of unselfish love.

The first angel is followed by a second who also has Good News but who warns against its clever counterfeit: "Another angel followed, saying, 'Babylon is fallen, is fallen.'" A third angel warns against a still more clever future counterfeit, the most subtle that the world has ever seen: worship of the beast and his image and receiving his "mark" (verses 9-11).

The pure recovered gospel is ready for the 21st century. The reason why it is called "the everlasting gospel" is that it concentrates into one brilliant beam the light of truth that has shone dimly through all past centuries.

The Book of Revelation encourages us to hope for the very best. This vast activity on earth is not in vain. Fruitage springs up—the raising up of a people worldwide of whom God can honestly say, "Here is the patience of the saints; here are those who keep the commandments of God and the faith of Jesus" (verse 12). In giving His Son for the world, the Father made an infinite investment. Now it will be seen that it pays off. Christ did not make His sacrifice in vain. A people are raised up who deeply appreciate it. The hopes and fears of untold billions of all ages are summed up in that final assurance of atonement effected and realized.

The text assures us that He will have a worldwide body of people who reflect the beauty of His character. Of themselves they will have no innate goodness, but as broken scraps of otherwise worthless mirror can dazzle one's eyes with the sun's rays, so each believer in Christ will beautifully reflect a facet of His perfect character.

If God "so loved the world that He gave His only Son" two thousand years ago, we can be sure that He still "so loves" the world of today that He will not permit any human soul to miss hearing in some way what the Good News is. The apostle Paul calls it "righteousness by faith," an effective motivation for a change of heart (Galatians 5:5, 6). That final display of truth is symbolized in Revelation as "another angel coming down from heaven, having great authority, and the earth was illuminated with his glory" (Revelation 18:1). The love of God, the cross of Christ, demand the imminent fulfillment of this prophecy. This is the next item on the world's agenda.

The Good News reveals three glorious truths: a God who is a Heavenly Father; a Savior who remains for all eternity a member of the human family, One with us; and a Holy Spirit who is the Spirit of Christ sent to "abide" or to stay with every human soul who welcomes His presence. A great personage like the president of our nation may seem close to us through the television or computer screen, but he remains a finite human being who actually can be close to only a handful in his inner circle. Christ is closer to us individually than any human being can be because He comes in the presence of the Holy Spirit. How can anyone be depressed if he or she will believe such Good News?

CHAPTER THREE

The Youthful Search for
Meaning in Life

Thoughtful young people can hardly be lackadaisical about their convictions. When religion makes sense to them, their devotion becomes all-out. But when it doesn't, they tend to throw everything to the winds.

Some keep up a profession of religion because of the momentum of family tradition for generations. Nominal Catholic, Protestant, or Jewish religious roots are respectable. But the "traditional" Christian youth living in today's ungodly society finds conflict when coping with the unique demands of Bible Christianity. The pressures of a secular world are severe enough, but when friends also disparage their Bible convictions, many sincere youth ask themselves if being committed Christians is worth all the trouble.

One church leader lamented: "Almost every thinking adult is concerned with the slippage among our adolescent members. Hand-wringing is common." Empty seats in the youth division and in the worship services all too often bear eloquent witness. Almost any church board can observe first-hand how serious is this hemorrhage of loyalty among youth. While some may preserve their ties to their church because their social life centers around it, this physical presence in the church can often mask a deep spiritual emptiness.

Here are some documented remarks of youth reared in Christian homes, about how they feel toward religion. Somehow they see it as Bad News. They could never say these things if they understood the New Testament "everlasting gospel" as genuine Good News:

"Dull, and it gets in the way."

"It's just a bunch of do's and don'ts."

"I don't have any feelings toward it."

"A ritual-type thing. Emotional ups and downs."[1]

Among those who are trying to hold on there is often deep spiritual frustration. It is too difficult to be good, they think. Following Christ in modern society seems to be an uphill struggle. Few have the guts to endure. Here are more typical remarks, recorded by Dr. Roger Dudley:

"I have a lot of work to do if I want to be saved."

"I wish I could be completely good, but it isn't always easy."

"I want to serve God, but I find it very hard."

"I couldn't go through life with all those do's and don'ts.
But I guess I have to if I want to go to heaven."[2]

The attitudes of youth are often the unmasked, tell-it-as-it-is attitudes of adults. Grown-ups usually see their own measure of devotion mirrored in their children. That's how the erosion of moral values is perpetuated. Something evil has poisoned life on this planet. Other comparable surveys of youth in public schools disclose that an alarming majority will not endure any sacrifice for moral or spiritual values.

To reproduce the all-consuming devotion to Christ that the New Testament talks about, we need some nutriment that is lacking in our standard spiritual dietary. The problem is not that today's youth are innately worse than previous generations; they suffer spiritual malnourishment.

Somewhere between the cradle and college, Christian youth have absorbed a fear-motivated idea of the gospel. And such fear does not hold them when temptation comes. They reason that a bird-in-the-hand pleasure is worth two in the heavenly future, and the fear of losing out on the thrills of this world eclipses fear of losing the world to come. Fear of hell and hope of reward in heaven are spectacular failures as effective motivations for youth.

Youth Are Not the Only Problem

Why is it that the closer we come to the second coming of Christ, the less we are motivated by the Good News about it? Why can't we

---

1. Roger Dudley, *Why Teenagers Reject Religion and What to Do About It*, Review and Herald Publishing Association, pp. 20, 21, 1978.
2. Ibid., pp. 9, 17.

catch the vision of that star that shone so brightly for the apostles, for the Reformers, and for the missionary pioneers of previous generations?

One answer is found in two distortions of Christianity which have come down for centuries through the avenue of church history. Both inject a poison into spiritual nourishment:

(1) One is the extremely rigid, authoritarian, toe-the-line cult of conformity to rules and high external standards. This high performance is understood as demanded on pain of a rejection slip in God's final judgment. The basic idea is that it is *hard* to follow Christ in a genuine way, and it is correspondingly *easy* to be lost. Youth often have the impression that teachers don't lose much sleep if the student flunks his finals; and they carry this idea over into their impressions of God. It seems that He also will hardly care if they flunk their great Finals at the end. He has done His part long ago, as the teacher has done his part in dishing out the course content, and now it's up to them to do their homework and shape up.

For many, this is the traditional "gospel." They often feel that they can't shape up, that the burden is too heavy. Whether or not their impression is a fair one is not our point; *this is what we have allowed them to pick up*, and this is what matters.

(2) The opposite extreme has become popular, especially in urban communities—a relaxed attitude of anything-goes liberalism. This downplays the necessity or even the possibility of true righteousness or obedience to God's holy law. It is impossible for anyone to keep it properly, says this view. Therefore He does not expect us to. Try to be moral if you can, but if it's not easy, trust His indulgent, grandfatherly softness. He will excuse you. "Occasional lapses" of moral failure are par for the course. Since Jesus is our Substitute, His perfect obedience always must be a cover-up to take the place of a mythical obedience that has never been possible for us. Serious-minded Christians have been naive to be so strict. So says this alternative "gospel."

Each of these two extremes is a protesting reaction against the other. And each produces confusion in the minds and hearts of youth. The traditional arch-conservative philosophy generates either resentment with rebellion, or pride if one imagines he measures up. The liberal philosophy generates unconcern because it ridicules time-honored high standards and implies that there is no future judgment for people who suppose they can't live up to them.

Youth Caught in the Cross-Fire of No-Man's Land

Pathetically, the sincere conservatives emphasize how difficult and nearly impossible is the path to heaven. Youth picture God as pointing out the steep path to salvation: "You want to go to heaven? It's a rough, rocky, thorny way; I hope you make it. Many people don't. I won't be surprised if you fail. If you do fail, I have someone else waiting to take your crown." Many feel that their absence from heaven would not be missed. Why bother to try? Why lose *both* worlds?

The opposite heresy of a careless abandon flaunts worldliness and sensuality in the face of divine warnings. But as surely as rigid traditionalism *drives* people away from Christ, so an "anything-goes" theology *entices* them away.

The pure New Testament gospel brings refreshing Good News. The problem can be corrected. With such an army as youth who are informed and challenged by the gospel in verity, the world can indeed be lightened with the glory of its message.

There is a cause for our general malaise of lukewarmness, our legalism and spiritual impotence. These problems are not inherent in the Bible message. *They are the consequence of a lethal perversion of it.* Some gigantic power in history has eclipsed the original gospel message and substituted a twisted version that has corrupted the world. This power is the mystic Babylon of Revelation (see Revelation 14:8; 16:19; 17; 18; cf. Daniel 7:19-26; 8:9-25).

This long campaign to twist and pervert the pure message of Good News has burdened the world with unnecessary agony. Both nature and the church abhor a vacuum. But "Babylon" has created a vacuum into which have rushed these alternative heresies of rigid traditionalism and loose liberalism. Both deny the essentials of the gospel message. Both are starved for its unique nutritive elements. Both extremes may battle on for decades; neither can win. And while the struggle drags on, there is no end to that stream of sincere youth who are confused and discouraged.

The New Testament gospel message presented an intensely interesting Christ as the true Leader of all who appreciate His Good

News. The apostles and early Christians sensed an empathy with Him that was all-absorbing. That union with Him is what many youth today have not seen. It's not their fault that the vision which shone so brightly in the apostolic message has been in a great degree denied them. We can't blame helpless people for being hungry and malnourished. It's time for us to hear some genuine Good News that supplies the missing motivation that works. More abounding sin demands much more abounding grace, and God has promised that He has it ready.

Why the New Testament Solution Is Effective

The New Testament message was supremely exciting, positive, and related to life. It kindled a "first love" experience in the hearts of those who heard it. There are definite reasons why its spiritual fruitage is still effective today:

(1) It tells the truth about the Lord whose love is active, not passive. Christ is seen as a Good Shepherd looking for His lost sheep rather than the lost sheep being left to seek for its Shepherd. Salvation does not depend on our holding on to God's hand but on our believing that He is holding on to our hand (Isaiah 41:13). In a very practical way which transcends theological hair-splitting, the gospel is a message of salvation by faith alone—a faith *which works*, not faith *and* works (Galatians 5:6; the Greek word is "energize").

(2) Christ is presented as a Savior "nigh at hand," not "afar off." This idea is refreshingly different from those held commonly in our day. The view that Christ took only the unfallen, sinless nature of Adam before the fall is a legacy of medieval Christianity that failed to appreciate how fully God became man in Christ. The opposite truth of Christ's nearness to us far transcends theological dispute: it is beautiful "practical godliness." As we shall see in chapter 10, the concept of "Christ's righteousness" is meaningless apart from the unique New Testament truth of His taking our fallen, sinful nature, yet remaining sinless and living a sinless life. He cannot truly be our Substitute unless He has truly taken our place as Immanuel, "God with us."

(3) Justification by faith is lifted above the realm of doctrinal hair-splitting and becomes a vital, throbbing message of union with Christ. Thus it supplies the motivation that makes the repentant, believing

sinner to become joyfully obedient to the law of God. Devotion ceases to be difficult, and self-sacrifice for Christ becomes a delight. If this truth is understood, the devotion to Christ displayed by the apostles becomes not only possible but certain, even in these decadent years of the twentieth-first century with its glittering rewards for me-first pleasure-seeking.

(4) The two covenants, a "doctrine" often regarded as a dry-as-dust theological bore, becomes a thrilling message of gripping interest. Paul's concept overcomes selfish motivation and activates the dormant capacity for love in hardened, apparently unfeeling hearts. The spiritual bondage of continual defeat and depression is seen to be the direct fruit of a widespread "old covenant" teaching that has mistakenly been assumed to be the "new covenant." Many who think they are too far gone, their hearts too cold ever to learn to "believe," sense tears welling up in their eyes as they discover spiritual power in the new covenant truth. (This will be discussed in chapter 11.) Again, "doctrine" transcends theology and becomes practical Christian living.

(5) The gospel cuts the Gordian knot of self-centered motivation underlying the blasé hypocrisy so nauseating to many youth. The pure New Testament idea creates a motivation of a heart-appreciation of the unique love of Christ that led Him to His cross. Through the utter simplicity of that message with its *enabling* demands and imperatives, it abolishes both the fear that discourages youth today and the boredom that wearies them. It also supplies the spiritual energy that fuels life-long devotion to Christ.

(6) Most of us find it impossible to read all of the Christian books published today. But what cannot be accomplished in a lifetime of deep study can happen in a very short time through grasping that message of more abounding grace. It imparts a hunger and thirst for the word of God that impels the believer in Christ to search the Bible and to understand it. No longer does he have to force himself to initiate and maintain a program of devotional reading or praying, any more than a healthy person must set his alarm clock in order to remember to eat his meals daily. A healthy appetite takes care of that problem!

The Heart Is Involved, Not Just the Head

A hope-inspiring hymn expresses something of the thrill of the message:

"Beauty for Ashes"

> I sing the love of Christ, my Saviour,
>   Who suffered upon the tree,
>   That in the secret of His presence,
>   My bondage might freedom be.
>
> He comes "to bind the broken hearted";
>   He comes the fainting soul to cheer;
>   He gives me "oil of joy" for mourning,
>   And "beauty for ashes" here.
>
> I sing the beauty of the Gospel
>   That scatters not thorns, but flow'rs.
>   That bids me scatter smiles and sunbeams
>   Wherever are lonely hours.
>
> The "garment of His praise" it offers
>   For "heaviness of spirit" drear;
>   It gives me sunshine for my shadow,
>   And "beauty for ashes" here.
>   —*J. G. Crabbe* (1889)

Youth of today who get a chance to hear the message sense the same phenomenal motivation gripping their hearts. The gnawing fear of the uncertain future or even of present-day terrorism melts away because the message recaptures the heart appeal of the New Testament and makes Christ's close identity with us to be realized. We can now more fully reproduce the New Testament evangel than even the message of the 16th century Reformers did, wonderful as that was.

On the other hand, the enticements of sensuality, appetite, wealth, the love of leisure and pleasure, the me-first mindset, the allurements of our scintillating electronic age, all lose their charm for the one who has seen that message of Christ's righteousness. Love of the world cannot survive in its penetrating light, and neither can conservative lukewarmness.

It is not that those who believe the Good News are made of sterner or better stuff than others. They have simply *seen something* that others have not yet seen.

Let us look.

CHAPTER FOUR

Christ's Second Coming: How Soon Is "Soon"?

Most Christians believe that Christ's second coming is near. That is good, for it is very true, more so than we think. But who *loves* the thought that it is near? Aside from some old or sick people, or prison inmates, who really want Him to come soon?

During the early part of the nineteenth century many humble Christians came to cherish such a desire. Members of different denominations, they discovered in the symbolism of Daniel and Revelation a prophetic road map which had not previously been clearly understood.

All churches had assumed for many centuries that these books were "sealed." But to these discoverers of prophecy, Daniel and Revelation came alive to focus the conviction that mankind's weary journey in this world of sin was about at its end.

While a few individuals scattered through the centuries had always spoken of the second coming of Christ as possibly near, no significant movement had ever before risen which clearly understood how a connected series of coherent Bible prophecies demonstrated that it was near.

It was as though the church had been sleeping like Rip Van Winkle for nearly 1800 years and suddenly awoke to a new experience—anticipating the imminent return of Jesus. This phenomenal new life

---

1. Daniel 7:25; 11:33-35; 12:4; Revelation 12:6, 14; 13:5. Almost without exception Bible scholars of all Protestant churches at that time recognized the "year-day" principle of understanding the time prophecies (Numbers 14:34; Ezekiel 4:6). The fact that Revelation repeats the 1260 days is evidence that they could not have been fulfilled literally in Old Testament times. Since both Daniel and Revelation are concerned with the coming conflict between Christ and Satan and describe it in symbols, it is obvious that the time periods are also symbolic.

followed the end of the prophetic period of 1260 years[1] when "the time of the end" began in 1798. This was great good news, and now these Christians began to share it.

You can imagine how these lovers of the Bible rejoiced to trace the "waymarks" on the prophetic road map. The thought of His return and the setting up of His kingdom was to them greater than the joy of winning the sweepstakes would be to us. The personal return of the beloved Savior in their lifetime was spoken of as the "blessed hope."

The reason why the news that a sinful world's journey was almost over was thrilling to them was not because they longed for relief from nineteenth century physical toil and privation, hard as that was, but because their hearts were in union with Christ. They cared about Him as a Person. They deeply appreciated His character of unselfish love. He was dearer to them than any human relationship. This was worship.

For these people there was no self-centered concern to cloud the bright flame of that devotion. In the over-sweep of the centuries which the book of Revelation pictures, they can be identified as the movement symbolized by the first angel's message of chapter 14:6, 7. This worldwide movement called upon "those who dwell on the earth" to "fear God and give glory to Him and worship Him that made heaven and earth."

A "First" Since Apostolic Times

This 1840s movement was the first time since the era of the apostles that Jesus could find a *community* of believers on earth whose hearts were knit with His in joyful expectation of His soon return. It was something as special as a bride's feeling for the bridegroom differs from that of the flower girl. They were among those of whom Jesus said, "Blessed are they that have not seen, and yet have believed" (John 20:29).

Devotion similar to that of the early Christians at Pentecost marked these pioneers. It leaped across the centuries like fire blown by the wind. One sea captain spent his life savings in spreading the message so that he came to face old age nearly penniless.[2] A college graduate gave up a promising career for the toil and privations of editing literature

---

2. Joseph Bates. See Mervyn Maxwell, *Tell It to the World*, Pacific Press (Boise, ID), pp. 74-84, 1976.

to spread the news. His sister prematurely burned out the strength of her youth.[3] Others sold farms and gave the proceeds to the cause. Young people threw themselves wholeheartedly into what came to be known as the Advent Movement. Some travelled overseas to endure hardship as pioneer missionaries, never thinking of personal reward. The taste of "the blessed hope" was in their "mouth sweet as honey" (see Revelation 10:9; this chapter describes the Advent experience).

The yellowed pages of their letters and journals testify to the joy they cherished in the "blessed hope." Revelation likens a bride's anticipation of union with her bridegroom to the thrill of the message that gave birth to the Great Second Advent Movement. The people who loved the message then were often ridiculed, but now many Christians profess to believe in the second advent (see Revelation 19:6, 7).

Cold theology and prosaic mathematics that unraveled Daniel's 2300 or 1290 "days" could never stir human hearts and emotions like that message did. They were about to welcome a Loved One who had been absent a long, long time. It was not superficial emotionalism, but a gripping experience that people in those days called "heart-work," the pure authentic joy of heart, the all-risking abandon, that some youth seek vainly in a drug-induced "high." Today's youth never attain it because they find only its jaded counterfeit. The Holy Spirit manifested His solemn presence in that Advent Movement, and the result was a sober, reasoned, lifelong "high" for those who saw the message in the Word.

All infatuation of illicit love, all idolatry even of valid human love, is a vain search for a reality that exists only in Christ. The mysterious charm that shines in an attractive human face is only a dim reflection of the light of His face. Romeo and Juliet die for a failure to see Him. Gilda sings her beautiful "Caro Nome" in *Rigoletto* to express her love for her Walter, not knowing that the only name that thrills forever is that of Jesus.

The youth who loved the thought of Christ's return needed no chemical dependency, no *affaire de coeur*,[4] to relieve soul-boredom. They knew first-hand the thrill that inspired Charles Wesley to sing, "Jesus, Lover of My Soul." They had rediscovered what the youthful

---

3. Ibid., pp. 95-105.
4. French, literally:"*matter of the heart*" meaning love affair.

Saul of Tarsus found on his way to Damascus, when a glorious light blinded his eyes and illuminated his soul forever after. Paul was never disobedient to the heavenly vision even until that day when he glimpsed sunlight for the last time as the headsman's axe fell. He bequeathed his joy "unto all them also that love His appearing" (2 Timothy 4:8).

This Love Affair With Christ Is True Christianity

The all-too-common motivation of fear of judgment and hope of personal reward in heaven is a pathetic distortion of the gospel. These youthful pioneers knew something of the phenomenal faith that gripped the hearts of apostolic Christians. Long before his day, the martyrs in the Roman Empire could have sung Isaac Watts' hymn:

> When I survey the wondrous cross
> On which the Prince of glory died,
> My richest gain I count but loss
> And pour contempt on all my pride.

> Were the whole realm of nature mine
> That were a tribute far too small;
> Love so amazing, so divine
> Demands my heart, my life, my all.

For these sincere believers to be with Jesus was heaven enough because their hearts appreciated the love that led Him to His cross. No sacrifice in difficult economic conditions was too much to make for truth. No missionary service, no exile of ministry in a lonely "dark" foreign land, was too arduous a deprivation. Calls to service elicited no questions about the pay, the perks, the climate, housing, or terms of service. Medical or retirement "benefits" never crossed their minds. Jesus said "Go ye!" and *fellowship with Him* was remuneration enough.

The thought of "the blessed hope" sustained them through trials that we find more difficult to endure as the nearness of the Lord's coming seems to recede from our "more enlightened" twentieth-first century vision. Our simplest conveniences and luxuries would have been unimaginable to them, yet the more we have, the less we seem to feel like consecrating to the Lord a portion of what we have.

Why are our human hearts so shriveled up, like an orange left on the shelf a long time? Are we losing the hope of Jesus' return?

People everywhere are asking, "Can we continue forever saying that the coming of Christ is 'soon'?" Why has time continued for so many decades after people began to realize that it "is near," and that "time is short"? Is it because we do not really want Him to come?

Why Christ's Coming Has Been So Long Delayed

There is a widespread idea that God has predetermined the time for Christ's second coming as a fixed date. Heaven's time clock has its peg firmly inserted in place, and all we can do is to exploit this world while we watch until the celestial mechanism triggers the time and here comes Christ in the clouds of heaven. This would mean that there is nothing those who follow Him by faith can do to hasten or to delay His coming. This idea is an outgrowth of Calvinism, the doctrine that emphasizes the sovereign predetermination of God's will.

There are statements from Jesus that seem to indicate that the time of the second coming is "conditional," that is, its fulfillment depends on the faithfulness of God's people. For example, Jesus told this parable:

> And He said, "The kingdom of God is as if a man should scatter seed on the ground, and should sleep by night and rise by day, and the seed should sprout and grow, he himself does not know how. For the earth yields crops by itself: first the blade, then the head, after that the full grain in the head. But when the grain ripens, immediately he puts in the sickle, because the harvest has come" (Mark 4:26-29).

In telling this parable, Jesus obviously intended to comment on the time of His return, because the same symbol appears in the picture of His coming in Revelation. Something important happens that makes it possible for Him to come at last:

> And I looked, and behold, a white cloud, and on the cloud sat One like the Son of Man, having on His head a golden crown, and in His hand a sharp sickle. And another angel came out of the temple, crying with a loud voice to Him who sat on the cloud, "Thrust in Your sickle and reap, for the time has come for You to reap, for the harvest of the earth is ripe" (Revelation 14:14, 15).

According to these passages, the actual time of Christ's second coming depends on the "harvest" getting ripe, that is, on God's people being ready for His coming. Obviously, He loves them too much to come if they are not ready! If He came when they were not ready, they would only be consumed by the brightness of His coming (2 Thessalonians 2:8). The issue hinges on that readiness.

This explains why His coming has been so long delayed beyond the time when His people have expected Him. It makes very good sense. But it can also widen still further the gap of prophetic credibility. If the prophecies that declare the end to be near are conditional on the faithfulness of God's people, what will happen if God's people forever go on being *un*faithful? Suppose they never really want to get ready? Will that doom the second coming?

This explanation, if not understood, can convey terribly bad news. So far, God's people have indeed been unfaithful. The history of ancient Israel, continually backsliding, has been repeated in modern Christian history. Because of our unbelief, time has continued far beyond what it should have. Will the end therefore never be truly near? How near is "near"?

Although Jesus tells us that no "angels which are in heaven" know the actual time of His second coming (Mark 13:32), the Bible does declare emphatically that when the prophetic scenario shall unfold as pictured in Daniel and Revelation, in those "days of the voice of the seventh angel, when he shall begin to sound, the mystery of God should be finished, as He hath declared to His servants the prophets." There shall "be time [delay] no longer" (Revelation 10:7, 6, KJV). Time cannot drag on and on indefinitely, or the honor and credibility of God Himself will be ruined.

The factor that makes the difference is what the Bible speaks of as "the latter rain" outpouring of the Holy Spirit.

Why the Latter Rain Differs from the Early Rain

That picture of the harvest getting ripe so that Christ can thrust in His sickle to reap is a beautifully expressive symbol. The One who went to the cross for us, who poured out His soul unto death, who suffered unspeakable agonies for our redemption, looks upon that ripened "grain" as the hard-won fruitage of all His sacrifice. He deserves a reward!

All of earth's thousands of years of history have been the growing season preparatory to this moment of harvest when He personally returns. Out of earth's billions of inhabitants of all ages there comes at last a remnant of precious souls who gladly receive the showers of the outpouring of the Holy Spirit. Only as that rain falls can the grain ripen. The mature faith of those who believe God's Word has at last produced in a community of believers a reflection of the beauty of Christ's character. That reproduction of His character is the fruit. Without fail, the great, grand work is to be accomplished of bringing out a people who will be able to stand in "the day of the Lord."

This is the practical godliness aspect of that ripening grain. Nothing happening anywhere in the world today is as important as this! Out of earth's billions, there will be a remnant of faithful ones who will not be ashamed when they see Christ at His return, and who will genuinely welcome Him. Neither will He be ashamed of them. Tons of ore have at last yielded an ounce of purest gold. Heaven rejoices that the sacrifice of Christ is fully rewarded in a people whose mature faith has demonstrated that Christ came to save His people *from*, not *in*, their sins. At last, the pure gospel of righteousness by faith has come into its own. The sacrifice on the cross and His High Priestly ministry have guaranteed this result.

Note that no one prepares himself or herself for the harvest. No grain can ever ripen by itself without being watered. Our part is to *welcome* that blessing, and not to fight it off and resist it. *The latter rain of the Holy Spirit's outpouring causes the grain to ripen.*

The *early rain* fell at Pentecost, and has been received ever since through the past 2000 years as untold multitudes of human souls have prepared for death. The figure is drawn from the Palestinian barley crop where the annual early and latter rainy seasons were familiar to farmers. The early rain enables the grain to sprout and to grow, but not to ripen for the harvest. The ripening is a change that can only be produced by the latter rain.

There must also come a spiritual change before Christ's second coming. A people must be prepared, not for death, but for translation without seeing death, because the Bible differentiates between the multitudes who have died believing in Christ and those who are living when He comes:

> I do not want you to be ignorant, brethren, concerning
> those who have fallen asleep, lest you sorrow as others who

have no hope. ... We who are alive and remain until the coming of the Lord will by no means precede those who are asleep. For the Lord Himself will descend from heaven with a shout, with the voice of an archangel, and with the trumpet of God. And the dead in Christ will rise first. Then we who are alive and remain shall be caught up ... in the clouds to meet the Lord in the air. And thus we shall always be with the Lord (1 Thessalonians 4:13-17).

I looked, and behold, a Lamb standing on Mount Zion, and with Him one hundred and forty-four thousand, having His Father's name written on their foreheads. ... And they sang as it were a new song before the throne, ... and no one could learn that song except the hundred and forty-four thousand who were redeemed from the earth. ... And in their mouth was found no guile, for they are without fault before the throne of God (Revelation 14:1-6).

The Lord says He is ready to work with each one on earth who is willing. A great outpouring of the Holy Spirit will accomplish a work that makes ready a worldwide community of believers for the coming of the Lord. It also empowers them to complete the great unfinished commission of proclaiming the everlasting gospel to all the world. Only those who are humble in heart, who feel a need, who "hunger and thirst for righteousness" by faith, can discern and receive this special gift of the Holy Spirit (cf. Matthew 5:6 and Revelation 3:14-19). All who feel arrogantly "rich and increased with goods" in their proud assumed possession of "salvation" will miss it. If you can imagine thirsty plants putting up umbrellas to keep off the rain, you can see the true attitude of Christians who don't want to receive Heaven's latter rain.

In the meantime, we can be sure that Christ is waiting with longing desire for the manifestation of Himself in His true people who love Him. When His character shall be perfectly reproduced in His people, then He will come to claim them as His own.

Praying for Something While We Resist It

Ancient Israel failed time and again. The Old Testament tells how they complained of God's leadership in bringing them out of Egypt, how they refused to enter the land of Canaan when Joshua and Caleb urged them to go in, how they later coveted a king like the nations around them, how their kings repeatedly slid back into idolatry and apostasy, how rulers and people finally became so corrupt that Jerusalem and the temple were destroyed by the Babylonians and the people were marched in bonds into captivity.

The supreme tragedy of unbelief came later when their descendants who had prayed for 2000 years for the coming of their Messiah rejected Him when He came. Christ's gospel commission could have been finished long before this if "modern Israel" had not resisted the latter rain gift of the Holy Spirit as our ancestors anciently rejected the Messiah. The gift is not emotionalism, but clearer truth.

Some today feel discouraged because they think that this syndrome of rejecting Heaven's blessing must continue on and on in the organized Christian church. But this is not, cannot be, true.

Because the kingdoms of Israel and Judah were unfaithful in ancient times and the Jews rejected Christ and the Christian church has done little better, they mournfully conclude that the church today has doomed itself to ultimate failure as well.

But there is a truth that these discouraged ones have overlooked. The Lord has staked His eternal honor on His word: "I will come again" (John 14:3). Since that promise cannot fail, neither can His people's preparation for His coming fail. That preparation is foretold in this prophecy: "Unto two thousand and three hundred days [years ending in 1844]; then shall the sanctuary be cleansed" (Daniel 8:14, KJV). The sanctuary is the center of God's saving activity in behalf of His people and the world. In the great cosmic struggle between Christ and Satan, the honor of God's throne is involved, and the sanctuary is where the issues must be resolved for victory.

Daniel's prophecy gives immense hope to Christians everywhere. Christ's honor will at last be fully vindicated through that heavenly sanctuary ministry. The plan of salvation will be demonstrated to be a success, and Satan will be forever defeated. There is bright hope ahead!

In the ancient Israelite sanctuary service, a symbol or type foreshadowed the true ministry of Christ as High Priest in the heavenly sanctuary. Part of that ancient symbolism was the Day of Atonement ministry of the high priest in the second apartment of the sanctuary.[5]

---

5. See Hebrews 7:9 for the New Testament application of the ancient typical sanctuary ministry to the antitypical heavenly ministry of Christ. Note that there is a difference between the ministry in the Holy Apartment and that in the Most Holy Apartment.

Every faithful Jew regarded the annual Day of Atonement in the Most Holy Apartment as a miniature Day of Judgment. (Orthodox Jews still regard it so.) Daniel's prophecy declares that an antitypical Day of Atonement is to begin at the end of the 2300 years.[6] Something is to happen in this cosmic sanctuary cleansing that has never happened before. And here we come to the mysterious parting of the ways between faith and unbelief. *Faith believes that prophecy of Daniel and cooperates with the great High Priest in His closing work in the cosmic Day of Atonement.* Unbelief rejects that truth. It is a refusal to follow Christ all the way.

Christ is our Savior; we cannot save ourselves even one percent. But we can *cooperate* with Him. We can stop resisting Him. We can *let* Him do His work for us and in us. Such faith will cease resisting the Holy Spirit's leading. It will motivate us to surrender to the cross whereon self is crucified "with Christ." Such a transformation is indeed a miracle, but such a miracle is what our great High Priest specializes in. Thus human selfishness is overcome.

God has chosen to exercise faith that His people will not fail Him (see Galatians 2:20; Romans 3:3, 4). The previously unending syndrome of unbelief and unfaithfulness that has prevailed for so many millennia will at last be broken.

Getting ready *while still alive* to meet the Judge of all the earth face to face when He returns personally the second time—this strikes terror to many stout hearts. Those who blithely dismiss this experience as nothing serious just haven't given thought to it. But "the everlasting gospel" of Revelation 14 is Good News sent to dissipate this fear and to prepare a people for the harvest.

From the time of the apostles down through the centuries to our day many honest, sincere hearts rejoiced to receive the gift of the Holy

---

6. The angel said to Daniel that at the end of the 2300 years, "then shall the sanctuary be cleansed." Moses knew that the earthly sanctuary was only a type or kindergarten representation of the "true tabernacle which the Lord erected, and not man" (Hebrews 8:2). Daniel also understood this. The heavenly sanctuary is the place where Christ ministers as High Priest. The ancient versions of Daniel support the King James Version and *The New King James Version* reading of "cleansed" in Daniel 8:14, thus demonstrating that the antitypical Day of Atonement ministry is meant (cf. Leviticus 16:29, 30). It is this final phase of Christ's High Priestly ministry that commenced in 1844 and continues until a people are made ready for His second coming.

Spirit, but it was always that of the *early rain*. During that time, there was no latter rain. The early apostles of the Lord would welcome the latter rain if they were alive today. A distinct line of demarcation exists between the early rain and the latter rain, and that dividing line is in these last days.

These truths of the sanctuary help us tremendously to understand the mystery of the long delay in the return of Christ. The faith of sincere Christians in His soon coming is not rustic naïveté. Holy Scripture does indeed support their convictions. The delay is not God's fault. True faith in Christ's closing work of atonement will resolve the confusion and make "soon" become *soon*.

Faith in Christ's Coming Is "Present Truth"

The apostle Peter reminds us that our understanding of the gospel must never become static but grow. We are to be "established in the present truth" (2 Peter 1:12). A preparation for the second coming of Christ is the movement that is to bring fruition to 2000 years of Christianity. It is to complete the arrested Protestant Reformation of the 16th century and recover the truths that even John and Charles Wesley in the 18th century could not quite fully perceive in their day, fervent as they were. The principle of God's leading is that He has reserved something better for us living in the last days (see the principle expressed in Hebrews 11:40).

The world stage in the 19th century was set for the end of the reign of sin and suffering. Events in the political world, the lineup of Islam, Catholicism, Protestantism, and paganism, were a perfect backdrop of the scenario of Daniel and Revelation. It is astounding but true that before the inventions of radio, TV, jet travel, and computers, it would have been easier and quicker to take "the everlasting gospel" to the whole world of that day than is our task now. Our most effective electronic presentations today are quickly drowned out by the never-ending flood of sophisticated entertainment often inspired by Satan. The proclamation of the gospel of Christ requires effective communication of one human heart to another, not merely visual or audio exposure to electronic stimuli.

To increase the difficulty, for many Christian people the entire prophetic picture of Daniel and Revelation has slipped out of focus. So vast and complex are the needs of world population for social betterment that many can now see only many years of "social gospel" work. For example, millions caught in chemical dependency and inadequate diet need physical deliverance before they can even begin to comprehend the gospel. Hundreds of millions, even billions, are so ground down by the economic struggle to survive in crowded urban and village existence that they can hardly "hear" the gospel message. But the Holy Spirit will provide the power to capture the attention of earth's billions. God's love requires it.

No one who is ready to welcome the Lord when He returns will be ashamed of himself in that day. As each one looks back on his life, he will be happy for the knowledge that he has devoted all he could of his time and strength to cooperating with Christ to help others get ready for that great event.

The Long Delay Intensifies Our Problem

To many of this generation, the Papacy no longer appears to be the "beast" of Daniel and Revelation, as Protestants of former generations understood. Now, they think, it must be some other world power. Prophetic certainties which were held by previous generations of Christians are meaningless to them. Discordant voices sometimes try to re-interpret Daniel and Revelation, usually contradicting each other, and all succeeding only in deepening the confusion.

Can we get the picture back into focus again?

Yes, by paying serious attention to what Jesus says. He urges us in these last days to be sure we "understand" those prophecies of Daniel (Matthew 24:15). In fact, Christ is the key to understanding them. Further, it is He Himself who equally urges us to give very special attention to Revelation: "Blessed is he who reads and those who hear the words of this prophecy" (Revelation 1:3). This is the "present truth" that is worth more than winning all the sweepstakes prizes in the world—understanding the gospel of the grace of Christ in the setting of His prophecies.

The reason why Jesus urged us to understand Daniel and the Revelation is that these prophecies reveal the truth about the great spiritual battle raging between Satan and Christ. The "fourth beast" of Daniel 7 and the "little horn" of chapter 8 aptly delineate the great world religious movement that professes to be Christian but in reality is baptized paganism. Revelation develops the same theme of that great cosmic controversy ending in a gigantic spiritual struggle in the last days. God's people will endure the final test of persecution and stand firm for Christ, "the Lamb," and prepare for His second coming. Only as we clearly distinguish between the true Christ and Satan's clever counterfeit, the false christ, can we be sure to avoid the most monstrous and fatal deception of all world history.

Could anything be more important than discovering that genuine Good News that unveils this deception and reveals the true Christ?

CHAPTER FIVE

If It Isn't Interesting, Maybe It Isn't True

The word "gospel" means "good news," and good news is always interesting. When Jesus proclaimed it, "the common people heard Him gladly" (Mark 12:37). The apostles' preaching was also so powerful and attractive that their enemies confessed that they had "turned the world upside down" (Acts 17:6).

In every age, God's Good News has compelled the attention of mankind. Never does the Holy Spirit indite a tame, lifeless message. The last proclamation of the gospel is communicated by angels "unto them that dwell on the earth, to every nation, and kindred, and tongue, and people, ... with a loud voice." Then the message swells "mightily" as it lightens the earth with glory (Revelation 14:6, 7, KJV; 18:1-4). The "angels" symbolize the ministry of God's servants.

This scenario calls for the most powerful and interesting communication that the world has ever heard. Neutrality is an impossible reaction to it. As in the days of the apostles, people will get off the fence and either accept it wholeheartedly or reject it just as decidedly.

Any presentation of the "gospel" that is dull and boring is suspect. The youth who complain that Christianity is not exciting, not positive, not attractive, most likely have never heard that pure gospel message which catalyzes humanity.

The full truth of the New Testament gospel message is the sweetest melody that can come from human lips—justification by faith, and the righteousness of Christ. Imagine a message so joyous and hope-inspiring that the listeners are tempted to think it is too good to be true. That is what people thought when they heard the Apostle Paul proclaim "glad tidings" (Acts 13:32).

The message is not so much the miracle of feeding hungry people as the greater miracle of developing a spiritual appetite in people who are so undernourished that they do not even feel hungry for the truth of God's word. The Lord wants us to learn to appreciate what a blessing a healthy appetite is. Without it, life is hardly worth living, and death by starvation may be the result.

Not only is the Lord our Shepherd, He is also our Host who seats us at His table loaded with nutritious spiritual food. But most of us are not spiritually hungry and thirsty, and many are literally starving for food for their souls. Day after day, week after week passes by without their personally eating the Bread of life. A millionaire starving for want of an appetite may be worse off than a famine refugee who feels his hunger.

Humanity is dying for the want of teaching on the subject of righteousness by faith in Christ, and on kindred truths.

The Inestimable Blessing of Feeling Hungry and Thirsty

There is a special happiness that comes to those who feel this spiritual appetite. Jesus says, "Blessed are those who hunger and thirst for righteousness, for they shall be filled" (Matthew 5:6). What kind of happiness will we know when we learn to feel that hunger?

Familiar truths of the Bible will present themselves to our mind in a new way; texts of Scripture that we may have learned in childhood will burst upon us with a new meaning. We will know that Christ Himself is leading us by His Spirit; a divine Teacher will be at our side.

Furthermore, we will no longer need to force ourselves to speak to someone else about our faith. We will sense a motivation to speak to others of the comforting things that have been revealed to us. We will want to communicate some fresh thought in regard to the character or the work of Christ. We will have some insight of His love to communicate to those who love Him and to those who do not love Him. The wisdom that enabled Jesus to reach all kinds of people can be communicated to the one who believes in Him, for He says that "greater works than these he will do, because I go to My Father" (John 14:12).

When the Lord says that we are "blessed" when we hunger after righteousness, what kind must He be speaking of? There is only one kind—that which is by faith. Not one human soul possesses even a tiny amount of innate, natural righteousness. The Bible says that "all alike have sinned," and "all the world [has] become guilty before God" (Romans 3:23, 3:19, NEB).

The first step in receiving the gift of real salvation is to realize and confess that we need it—totally. Christ is not a Repairman who patches us up a bit. Those who are converted are created anew, given a new heart (John 3:3-8; Psalm 51:10; Ezekiel 36:26).

In other words, those who feel that they already understand righteousness by faith lose the blessing, while those who feel empty are the only ones who can "be filled." This is a tragic reality, for there are even some ministers and church leaders who do not sense their need and have no appetite. They already feel "full," when they are starved.

According to the Lord Jesus, we, both leaders and people, have a basic general problem. Speaking especially to the leaders of His people in the last days, He says: "You say, 'I am rich, have become wealthy, and have need of nothing'" (Revelation 3:16, 17). This is another way of saying, "You say, 'I don't feel hungry or thirsty.'" The Lord is describing how His people generally feel wealthy in their understanding of the gospel, when in reality they are desperately "poor." "We have the truth; we understand the doctrine of righteousness by faith," is their boast. This feeling of satisfaction dooms us to world embarrassment, for He says that we are "wretched, and miserable, and poor." There is little in such Christianity to make the world take notice.

And, says the Lord Himself, the ones who *primarily* exhibit this lack of healthy appetite are the leadership of His people in the last days.[1] The "angel of the church" is not the same as the church itself. The churches are "the seven golden candlesticks," but "the angel of the church of the Laodiceans" is its leadership, including administrators, educators, pastors, elders, deacons, teachers, youth leaders, etc. As a group, the Lord says we share that common illness of feeling full when in fact we are malnourished.

---

1. Verse 14; Revelation 1:20. "The church of the Laodiceans" is the seventh, the last of the long series extending from the time of the apostles down to the end of world history. Thus Laodicea in Revelation is obviously the church of our present day. "The angel of the church" is the leadership of the church. According to Christ in Revelation 3:14-21, that is where the basic problem of the church has its source.

He is not criticizing or finding fault with us; He is a Physician who tells the patient the truth that he has cancer and only immediate surgery will save his life. This is a message of love, for only those whom He loves with intimate family love (*phileo*) does He "rebuke and chasten" (Revelation 3:19).

A Message of Healing for the Church

In former times, faithful ministers pleaded with God that the haughty hearts of church members might realize and feel deeply the meaning of redemption, and seek to learn the meekness and lowliness of Jesus. In all churches there are serious-minded people who sense that something is wrong. They feel deeply that a revival of true godliness is the greatest and most urgent of all our needs. They see pride in the church, hypocrisy, deception, vanity of dress, frivolity, and amusement. They see a desire for supremacy. All these sins can cloud the mind so that eternal realities cannot be discerned.

Even though we now sense a lack of revival and reformation, there are beautiful pictures of success that describe the future of God's work. "This gospel ... will be preached in all the world," says Jesus confidently. "The earth will be filled with the knowledge of the glory of the Lord, as the waters cover the sea." "I will pour out My Spirit on all flesh; ... It shall come to pass that whoever calls on the name of the Lord shall be saved. For in Mount Zion and in Jerusalem there shall be deliverance" (Matthew 24:14; Revelation 18:1-4; Habakkuk 2:14; Joel 2:28-32).

Jesus likened His people to "wineskins" that cannot hold "new wine" unless they are also made new (Matthew 9:17). If through faith in Christ we will become new "wineskins," He will fill us with the "new wine" of precious New Testament truth. God will give additional light, and old truths that have long been lost will be recovered and replaced. One interest will prevail, one subject will swallow up every other—the pure, unadulterated gospel of "CHRIST OUR RIGHTEOUSNESS" (see Jeremiah 23:6; 33:16; Isaiah 32:17).

This last message is to be simple, beautiful, and always interesting. The future in God's plan has to be Good News. As we discover what that most precious message is, we shall find that it differs from what is commonly assumed to be "the doctrine of righteousness by faith." We shall find that popular ideas outside of the Bible have infiltrated our thinking so that Christ seems far away and distantly unconcerned about us. The truth about Him is Good News far better than most people imagine is possible. The revelation of "Christ our righteousness" discloses Him as a Savior nigh at hand and not afar off.

How Can We Learn to Feel Hungry and Thirsty?

Seldom can a sick person be healed by forced feeding, although in emergencies it may be necessary. To grit your teeth and clench your fists and force yourself to read the Bible and pray may possibly be helpful, but it is doubtful. A healthy person does not eat two or three meals a day because the Bible tells him to or because the doctor orders him to. He eats because he is hungry; his appetite drives him to it.

That hunger is what the true gospel activates in a believing person's heart. If the hunger is not there, the reason has to be one or the other of two problems: (1) he or she has not understood how good the Good News is; or, Heaven forbid! (2) he or she has rejected it.

For example, the Lord says:

> To you who fear My name the Sun of Righteousness shall arise with healing in His wings; and you shall go out and grow fat like stall-fed calves (Malachi 4:2).

Note that the "healing" activates the growth! To "fear" His name does not mean to be afraid that He will zap you if you don't shape up. It means to reverence His character; and that becomes possible only when you see and appreciate His goodness; and again, that in turn depends on comprehending what happened at His cross. All this is the "healing" process.

This is precisely the experience that true faith in Christ accomplishes. Our natural, unconverted heart is "enmity against God," or alienated from Him (Romans 8:7). But the love revealed at the cross heals that alienation:

> All things are of God, who has reconciled us to Himself through Jesus Christ, and has given us the ministry of reconciliation, that is, that God was in Christ reconciling the world to Himself, not imputing their trespasses to them, and has committed to us the word of reconciliation. Therefore we are ambassadors for Christ, as though God were pleading through us: we implore you on Christ's behalf, be reconciled to God. For He made Him who knew no sin

to be sin for us, that we might become the righteousness of God in Him (2 Corinthians 5:18-21).

Elsewhere Paul calls this experience "receiving the reconciliation" (Romans 5:11). To return to Malachi's illustration of the calves in the stall, a process of growth begins immediately, and growth is always characterized by a healthy appetite. Calves that are growing up can't get enough food! You don't have to force them to eat.

Something is wrong if we have to force ourselves to read the Bible and pray. A buried root of alienation from God is still there in the heart. Something is wrong if husband or wife has to force himself or herself to spend time with each other. "Husband, wife, I've made a New Year's resolution: I'm going to try to force myself to spend ten or fifteen minutes with you each day, and I hope I can remember, because if I don't I am afraid I'll suffer some disaster." How does the Lord feel when we have to set our alarm clocks and discipline ourselves in order to remember to spend some time with Him and His word? What has happened to the appetite, to the natural hunger that love inspires?

As "the power of God to salvation," the pure gospel reconciles the alienated heart to God through the blood of the cross, implanting a hunger for the word of God and a yearning to talk with the Lord that can never be fully satisfied until we meet Him face to face. As physical hunger drives one to eat, so reconciliation with God, or receiving the atonement, motivates us to search the Bible hungrily.

Paul says that he finds his greatest delight "in the cross of our Lord Jesus Christ, by whom the world has been crucified to me, and I to the world" (Galatians 6:14). That means that the attractions that the world once exercised upon him had lost their appeal. Silly TV entertainment and worldly pleasure that once engrossed our attention become nauseating. We have tasted something infinitely better. The heart is captivated by truth!

Eat a delicious peach, or grapefruit, or pear, or some strawberries, and you will find that a candy bar no longer tastes as good as you once thought it did. Jeremiah's experience will become yours: "Your words were found, and I ate them, and Your word was to me the joy and rejoicing of my heart" (Jeremiah 15:16).

Is there never a time for force-feeding? Yes, perhaps, but only as an emergency measure. This new experience of at-one-ment is something which *the Lord* has initiated, for it was He "who has reconciled us to

Himself." He also seeks to maintain it. Note the following that speaks of Christ's experience; it will also become yours if you do not resist:

> The Lord God has given Me the tongue of the learned, that I should know how to speak a word in season to him who is weary. He awakens Me morning by morning, He awakens My ear to hear as the learned, The Lord God has opened My ear; and I was not rebellious, nor did I turn away (Isaiah 50:4, 5).

Christ's love is active, not merely passive. He is not aloof, telling us, "Take it or leave it!" He takes us by the hand to lead us: "For I, the Lord your God, will hold your right hand" (Isaiah 41:13). Don't resist His leading or turn away! Jesus promised that He would send the Holy Spirit as His Vicar "that He may abide with you forever" (John 14:16). It is He who awakens us "morning by morning" to listen, to study, to "eat" the word. "Your ears shall hear a word behind you, saying, 'This is the way, walk in it.'" (Isaiah 30:21).

Make it your choice to respond to His "awaking," His prompting. Let David's response be yours: "When You said, 'Seek My face,' my heart said to You, 'Your face, Lord, I will seek'" (Psalm 27:8).

Peter talks about this keen appetite which is generated within us by the Holy Spirit: "As newborn babes, desire the pure milk of the word, that you may grow thereby, if indeed you have tasted that the Lord is gracious" (1 Peter 2:2). This is not only a command; it is a promise of the unending happiness your fellowship with the Lord will bring. It all comes about by *tasting* that the Lord is gracious.

That's why this book has been written, an attempt to activate that "taste." From then on, the appetite will take care of itself!

This is not to suggest that haphazard impulses are the way to study the Bible and to converse with the Lord in prayer. Our meals are not haphazard; we have regular times set aside and we do not resent taking time out from work or play in order to eat. Plan for a time for daily devotional visits with the Lord and His word. The original language of Isaiah 55:6 reads thus:

> *Pay attention to the Lord* while He may be found, call upon Him while He is near. Let the wicked forsake his way, and the unrighteous man his thoughts; let him return to the Lord, and He will have mercy upon him; and to our God, for He will abundantly pardon.

How can anyone resist that divine initiative?

CHAPTER SIX

If It Isn't Good News, It Can't Be True

God loves beautiful things, and we can learn to appreciate them, too. What a pity to be blind and deaf to the glory of God's creation!

We can know some of the thrill of appreciating beauty; but can we feel the greater thrill of appreciating the glory of His message of salvation? Is the gospel a system of abstract theology as impersonal as the science of mathematics or chemistry? If so, we do have to force ourselves to feed on it, for no heart-hunger could then be possible! Is making sure of salvation a cold business-like process of commitment like taking out an insurance policy?

The true gospel is fantastically beautiful, a *message* that grips the human heart more deeply and more lastingly than any human love could do. Straight-forward New Testament truth seems fresh and different to many who hear it. It seems shocking to them to realize that Jesus said there is only one prerequisite to salvation: "God so loved the world that He gave His only begotten Son, that whoever believes in Him should not perish but have everlasting life" (John 3:16.) According to this, our part is to *believe*. (The Greek word for "believe" and "to have faith" is the same.) Thus Jesus taught clearly that salvation is by faith, and since He added nothing else, He obviously meant that salvation is by faith alone.

That makes us draw a deep breath. Isn't it necessary to keep the commandments, to pay tithe, give offerings, keep the Lord's day, and do good works, *ad infinitum*? Yes, but we have no right to add to John 3:16 words that He did not utter.

Then did Jesus teach the "only believe!" heresy that lulls so many people into a do-nothing-and-love-the-world deception? No; He taught the kind of "faith *which works*," and which itself produces obedience to all the commandments of God. Such faith makes the believer "zealous of good works" so numerous that they cannot be measured (Galatians 5:6; Titus 2:14). God has already done the *loving*, and the *giving*. Our *believing* comes by responding to that Good News with the kind of appreciation that is appropriate—the yielding of ourselves and all we have to Him. The *ad infinitum* works follow such genuine faith as surely as fruit follows seed-planting.

It is a tragic mistake to assume that the true gospel message is soft on works. Pure righteousness by faith is the only message that can produce anything other than "dead works."

The Dimensions of the Love Poured Out at the Cross

What was the measure of the Father's love? Note carefully that verb in John 3:16: "God so loved ... that He gave His only begotten Son." He did not merely *lend* Him. He *gave* Him.

In our human judgment it is easy to assume that Jesus was *lent* to us as a missionary or foreign diplomat who spent 33 years in lonely exile on this planet and then returned to the luxury and security of His heavenly home-base. The agony of the cross lasted only a few hours, and the entire episode of His life on earth seems like a comparatively brief term of service, like a diplomat temporarily serving in a foreign post. But this idea is not true.

The reality of that sacrifice means infinitely more than most Christians imagine. The refreshing, wider view gives a glimpse of truth that melts the hard heart of anyone who will look and appreciate it.

When Jesus came to this earth as our Savior, He came from heaven where His "goings forth have been from of old, from everlasting" (Micah 5:2). He was always the divine Son of God, so that it was already a great sacrifice for Him to leave heaven and come to this dark world to suffer and die for us. But He gave even more. Paul speaks of seven steps of condescension that He took:

> Christ Jesus, ... being in the form of God, did not consider it robbery to be equal with God, but made Himself of no reputation, taking the form of a servant, and coming in the likeness of men. And being found in appearance as a man, He humbled Himself and became obedient to the point of death, even the death of the cross (Philippians 2:5-8).

Nothing in Scripture suggests that this was a loan for only 33 years. It was an eternal sacrifice. For all eternity He *gave* Himself to us. He bears our nature forevermore. He stepped down lower than the angels. He is forever our Brother. That truth begins to reveal the dimensions of the love that led Him to die for us.

Whether one believes it or not, there is a subduing power in it, and the heart must stand in silence in the presence of that awe-inspiring fact. Whenever that blessed truth comes to us that the sacrifice of the Son of God is an eternal sacrifice, and *all for me*, our heart-response must be like that of the ancient king of Israel who "went softly" before the Lord after his heart became repentant (Ahab, 1 Kings 21:27).

To *believe* therefore means to appreciate that immeasurable love, to stand in awe of it, to *let* your human heart be moved by it to the place where you forget yourself and your petty human desires and ambitions, and you *let* that love motivate you to a devotion you never dreamed was possible for you to feel. Righteousness is not by faith and works; it is by a "faith *which works*" (Galatians 5:6).

But we have a problem. How can we learn to appreciate that love, so that this powerful faith can begin to work in us? Is there more to that love than we have yet seen?

Why the Message of the Cross Is Powerful

The answer to our question lies in comprehending the kind of sacrifice that Jesus made on the cross. Paul finds his greatest delight in it because its reality solves a problem that all the psychiatrists and counselors in the world are powerless to solve: the problem of deep self-centeredness. "*I* have been crucified with Christ," he says (Galatians 2:20). The Greek word is *ego*. Here the gospel penetrates to the most fundamental element of humanity's universal psychosis.

Paul is not talking about a severe kind of self-hate. He saw a dynamic power in the cross that most of us have never seen. And because we haven't seen it, we can't help but remain self-centered and complacent in our supposed devotion to the Son of God who gave Himself for us. The very life we now enjoy was bought by His sacrifice, whether or not we believe and appreciate it. For those who do appreciate it and thus "believe," deliverance from the tyranny of self takes place, and for them He has also purchased eternal life (2 Timothy 1:10).

What is so special about Jesus dying for us? Billions of people have died, and many have suffered physical agony for longer periods of time than He did. Is the difference only in the personhood of the Victim—He was divine (whereas we who die are human), so that His death has sufficient value to satisfy the legal demands of the law?

However true this forensic concept may be, it does not do justice to the cross of Christ.

When He humbled Himself "even to the death of the cross," He suffered what Paul calls "the curse of the law, having become a curse for us (for it is written, 'Cursed is everyone who hangs on a tree')." The apostle is quoting the great Moses, who ruled that any criminal sentenced to die on a tree is automatically "accursed of God." That is, God has slammed the door of heaven against him and refused to hear his prayers for forgiveness (read Philippians 2:5-8; Galatians 3:13; Deuteronomy 21:22, 23). The criminal must suffer the utmost pain of emotional distress caused by complete despair. Don't get hung up on whether or not this was fair. Moses said it, and everybody believed it. That "curse" did not apply to other means of execution such as beheading or stoning.[1]

This is why a crucifixion was a gala event to watch, like a circus. The victim was God's write-off to be tormented as everyone's sadistic urges might dictate. If you as the spectator are "godly," this means you must show that you agree with God's judgment against him and curse him too, and do all you can to add to his torment. If you don't hate and revile the poor wretch on the cross, according to Moses you show that you are at odds with God.

As Christ hung on His cross, that's how the people viewed Him. They thought it was their duty to revile Him. Don't say that He was too smart and well-informed to let that "curse" bother Him. Paul adds that God "made Him who knew no sin to be sin for us" (2 Corinthians 5:21). He felt that curse which was ours by right, and it killed Him.

The Bible speaks of two different kinds of death, and we must not misunderstand the kind that Christ died. What we call death the Bible calls "sleep," but the real thing is called "the second death" (1 Thessalonians 4:13-15; Revelation 2:11; 20:14). It is the death in

---

1. No one knows whether in pre-Christian times some crucified victims did exercise faith in the coming Savior. If so, the curse would have been lifted from their souls, for they would have sensed a hope in Christ as "the Lamb slain from the foundation of the world" (Revelation 13:8). Surely the believing thief crucified with Christ knew that hope (see Luke 23:39-44).

which the sufferer sees not a ray of hope because he feels utterly forsaken by God, the horror-filled sense of utter darkness, the unspeakable pain of divine condemnation beyond which the sufferer can expect no vindication, no resurrection, no hope.

More than this, it is the death wherein one feels the full weight of sin's guilt, the fire of self-condemnation and total self-abhorrence burning in every cell of one's being. Such a person can have no feelings of innocence. Such a death is the curse that Moses mentioned. Since the world began, not one human soul has as yet died that "second death" or suffered the full consciousness of that complete God-forsakenness—with the exception of Jesus. This is why He was "made a curse for us" (Galatians 3:13, KJV). Even the thousands of crucified victims in Roman times were spared that full consciousness of darkness that Jesus felt, for He has always been "the true Light which gives light to every man who comes into the world" (John 1:9).

No one else has ever been physically or spiritually capable of feeling the full weight of that guilt of sin or sensing the full realization of the glory of a forfeited heaven. Not even our celebrated serial murderers who occasionally go to the electric chair have as yet died "the second death." No lost human being *can* feel this full load so long as the heavenly High Priest continues to serve as mankind's Substitute, for He is still "the propitiation … for the sins of the whole world" (1 John 2:2).

The Bible gives us a unique insight into the nature of Christ's death. In recently re-reading three major works by capable scholars on the nature of *agape* I was impressed that not one of them sees the deeper insight that the Apostle Paul saw in the cross. According to his insight, our Savior could not see through the tomb. When He cried out, "My God, My God, why have You forsaken Me?" He meant it. This was no actor's script to be recited on cue. Hope did not present to Him His coming forth from the grave a conqueror, or tell Him of the Father's acceptance of His great sacrifice. Isaiah says that "He poured out His soul unto death" (Isaiah 53:12). Christ felt to the full the anguish which a sinner would feel if mercy should no longer plead for the guilty race.

A Love That Surpasses Knowledge

In Ephesians 3:14-19 we can try to measure some of the dimensions of the love revealed at the cross as Paul saw them:

I bow my knees to the Father of our Lord Jesus Christ ... that you, being rooted and grounded in love, may be able to comprehend with all the saints what is the width and length and depth and height—to know the love of Christ which passes knowledge, that you may be filled with all the fullness of God.

(1) Paul is not concerned about our *doing* this or that, but he prays that we might *comprehend* something. He knows that if we grasp what the cross means, a new motivation will possess our hearts, and all the right-doing will then surely take place, even the good things that we have always felt we could not do. Bible study and prayer become a pleasure. Even sacrifice will become a delight.

(2) For Christ to dwell in our hearts by faith requires that we be "rooted and grounded in love [*agape*]." This is another way of defining faith as a heart-appreciation of that love.

(3) The dimensions of this love are as high as heaven, as deep as hell, as broad as the human race, as far away as your heart need or anybody else's.

(4) It is possible for us now to know "by faith" what "passes knowledge." Don't wait until eternity to begin to appreciate it! Without already stretching your mind and heart to "comprehend" it, you may not even begin to enter in to eternal life. Eternal life is not a materialistic, sensual orgy such as many Muslims imagine heaven to be; it begins now with a new spiritual awareness.

Our human hearts are so little and so shrunken up with love of self and love of the world that the simple story of the cross almost sweeps over our heads. Our tiny hearts need to be enlarged, as David prays, "I will run in the way of Your commandments, for You shall enlarge my heart" (Psalm 119:32).

(5) Someone very important, even the apostle Paul, prayed for you and me that we might join "all the saints" in comprehending this precious reality. The answer to Paul's prayer is the penetration of the gospel message to our awareness. It solves the problem of our universal love affair with our ego.

Why Has This Truth Not Been Understood as It Deserves?

Satan knows that if human beings can appreciate the dimensions of that love revealed at the cross, they will "be filled with all the fullness of God," as Paul prays (Ephesians 3:19). Hence the enemy wants to eclipse or to becloud it.

This has been the principal work of the "little horn" of Daniel 7 and 8 and the "beast" and "Babylon" of Revelation (Daniel 8:9-13; 7:25; Revelation 13:1-8; 14:8; 17). Long ago in the first centuries, this apostate power sought to corrupt this true idea that is essential to righteousness by faith.

Perhaps his most successful method has been to invent the doctrine of the natural immortality of the human soul, because he has nearly the whole world believing it. The idea came from paganism and was adopted by Christians of those early centuries who drifted away from New Testament teaching.[2]

This falsehood has had a devastating effect on righteousness by faith, for it neutralizes it. The modern complacency that pervades the world church comes from popular false concepts of the gospel that are related to this pagan idea. (Immortality is in Christ alone, bestowed at the resurrection. It is not innate, apart from Christ. The lost will never have it.)

We can easily see how this idea works to combat true faith. If the soul is naturally immortal, Christ could not have died for us! In fact, if the soul is naturally immortal, there can be no such thing as death, and Paul was wrong to say that "Christ died for our sins according to the Scriptures" (1 Corinthians 15:3). Christ's glorious sacrifice is automatically reduced to a few hours of physical and mental suffering

---

2. The Bible teaches that man's nature is mortal and that God "alone has immortality" (1 Timothy 6:16). Immortality resides in Christ and will be conferred upon believers at His coming when "this mortal must put on immortality" (1 Corinthians 15:53-55). What we call death Jesus called "sleep," saying that "'our friend Lazarus sleeps.' … Then Jesus said to them plainly, 'Lazarus is dead'" (John 11:11, 14). Paul also speaks of the dead as "those who sleep in Jesus": "The Lord Himself will descend from heaven with a shout … and the dead in Christ will rise first. Then we who are alive and remain shall be caught up together with them in the clouds to meet the Lord in the air. And thus we shall always be with the Lord" (1 Thessalonians 4:14-17).

while He was sustained by hope. Thus the pagan-papal doctrine dwarfs "the width and length and depth and height" of Christ's love. It reduces His *agape* to the dimensions of a human love which is motivated by self-concern and hope of reward.

False Ideas Produce a Weak Experience

The result is a diluting of the idea of faith to an egocentric search for security—a search for reward in heaven. The highest motivation possible remains likewise *ego*-centered. All pagan religions are self-centered in their appeal. And very few Christian churches can overcome this pagan-papal doctrine of natural immortality.[3]

Despite their great sincerity, so long as human minds are blinded thus they cannot appreciate the dimensions of the love revealed at the cross, and in consequence cannot fully appreciate true New Testament righteousness by faith. The result has to be a widespread lukewarmness, a spiritual pride, self-satisfaction, and subservience to *ego*-centered-ness. Fear always lurks beneath its surface as a motivation. The obverse side of the coin, hope of reward, is equally a motivation of self. When we distort faith itself to become egocentric, the gospel is paralyzed.

As best he could in his day, Luther understood this dynamic of faith as a heart-appreciation of *agape*, yet he fell short of a fully adequate grasp of its full dimensions. And after his death his followers soon reverted to the pagan-papal concept of natural immortality. Most popular ideas of justification by faith are conditioned by this concept. This is not to deny that some individuals manifest a sincere devotion to Christ while they assume the false teaching of natural immortality, but some exceptions only prove the rule. Whenever any pagan idea infiltrates the church in general, a general loss of zeal for Christ is the sure result.

The New Testament gospel begins to cut the ties that have bound us to these bankrupt views, to rediscover what Paul and the apostles saw. The three angels' messages of Revelation 14 foretell this recovery of truth.

Let us penetrate deeper into the New Testament idea of Good News.

---

3. See Appendix A, "Natural Immorality: A Key Deception," by Alexander D. Snyman, p. 127.

CHAPTER SEVEN

If You Can't Understand It, It Isn't the Gospel

There are two opposite mistakes that are commonly made concerning the gospel message:

(1) Many assume that it is the same message they have heard all their lives in church and revivals. Almost everybody believes it and nobody except atheists or Communists seriously opposes it. Ho-hum. A renewed interest in the gospel message is like re-inventing the wheel. Why the excitement?

(2) The opposite error is to assume that because the gospel is different, it must be a difficult, complex theological puzzle that few can unravel.

Both ideas are wrong. A little thought can readily show why.

(1) Revelation pictures "the everlasting gospel" going "to every nation, tribe, tongue, and people ... with a loud voice," and triumphing in a final movement that has "great authority" and illuminates "the earth" with "glory" (Revelation 14:6-12; 18:1-4). Of the 7.7 billion people on the planet, five billion are not Christians at all, and of those who claim to be, only a small percentage seem to demonstrate the fruit of the gospel—changed lives. Many who profess to be Christians assume that their righteousness by faith "doctrine" is the same as that taught in the Bible. But Revelation also reveals Christ as telling His church in our day that they are "poor" when they imagine themselves to be "rich" (Revelation 3:14-17).

If we were indeed "rich" in our understanding of the gospel, wouldn't the world have heard its message by now? Paul says that "the gospel ... is the power of God to salvation." It once turned the "world upside down" when it was proclaimed in its purity (Romans 1:16; Acts 17:6).

This chapter is to demonstrate also that (2) cannot be true. The message is simple; even a child can understand it. The only difficulty is that our deep human pride must be laid aside. Genuine righteousness by faith always lays the glory of man in the dust, including the glory that teachers and preachers find so tempting.

The history of God's dealings with His people proves that He "has chosen the foolish things of the world to put to shame the wise. ... And the things which are despised God has chosen, and the things which are not, to bring to nothing the things that are, that no flesh should glory in His presence" (1 Corinthians 1:27-29).

A child can see and understand the clear difference between genuine righteousness by faith and its clever counterfeits; the wise in their own eyes cannot. It is only those who "hunger and thirst after righteousness [by faith]" that *can* be filled (Matthew 5:6).

The Basic Difference Is Motivation

There are three motives that are generally employed to lead people to become Christians:

(1) *The desire to secure a reward in heaven.* All of us naturally want a place there. This motive is not evil, but neither is it effective, because it is not lasting. Satan can find a way to make us forget that ambition. If hope of reward is the reason why we are serving Christ, the deceiver will invent a temptation that eventually overrides that desire. He knows that we have a price and he will keep bidding until he gets us to cave in. We will sell out for some self-centered motivation, perhaps terror-inspired, preferring "a bird in the hand" of supposed carnal security to "two in the bush" of God's promises.

(2) *The fear of being lost in hell.* This is the other side of the same coin. It is natural also for us to feel this. "Through fear of death" we are "all [our] lifetime subject to bondage" (Hebrews 2:15). This motive is also not evil, but neither can it produce a truly unselfish character. It too will fail under strong, alluring temptation. Knowing that we have an ultimate "price," Satan can present a temptation so rooted in a more immediate fear that it will cancel out the future fear of being lost.

This will at last be the terrible "mark of the beast" test (see Revelation 13:11-18; 14:9, 10). There is a danger that multitudes of superficial Christians will succumb unless they get spiritual help. This is the reason for the special message of the "third angel" of Revelation 14.

(3) *The desire for personal benefits here and now.* This also is natural and understandable. And if the presentation is skillful, "selling God" like clever salesmen who supply the customers' needs can produce evangelistic results that appear good for here and now. But again, this motivation can produce nothing more in devotion than we see in contemporary popular religion. Even if we baptize a billion more people with this motivation, we will not hasten the coming of the Lord because it cannot prepare a people for His return.

The Source of Lukewarm Devotion

It is these motives that produce for now a "Laodicean" lukewarmness of devotion, and in the end will motivate us to sell out to our very clever enemy when he invents his final temptation. This final judgment will be severe, when multitudes who have heretofore appeared to be genuine grain prove to be chaff blown away by the wind (cf. Jeremiah 23:28; 1 Corinthians 3:11-15).

Evangelists can be salespersons whose technique is borrowed from popular business methods: develop in your prospect a sense of need and then convince him that he must buy your product in order to satisfy that need; show him how your product will satisfy his self-centered concern. In defense of this motivation, it can be said that it has often been employed in the past, even in Bible times. *But that does not mean that it will prepare a people for Christ's return.*

Can we not see what happens? The center of concern always remains *self*, that troublesome *ego*. Subsequent appeals to look from self to Jesus become vain words. "Looking to Jesus" always remains tied to this radius of *ego*-concern and insecurity. Thus the deep root of fear is not cast out; it is only buried deeper.

In contrast, the motive to which the New Testament gospel appeals is a cross-inspired faith. It is a "more excellent way." Paul tells the Galatians that in his preaching "Jesus Christ was clearly portrayed among you as crucified." Their response was phenomenal. As they listened, their ears were turned into eyes and they appreciated the significance of the Son of God dying for them. This was "the hearing of faith" (1 Corinthians 2:1-4; Galatians 3:1-5). Paul had learned a bitter lesson in his near-failure ministry in Athens. When he came to Corinth, he "determined not to know anything among you except Jesus Christ and Him crucified."

The apostles began with a presentation of *God's deed* in the sacrifice of the cross, and not with *man's need* of personal security. Thus they could by-pass the usual *ego*-centered motivations of the human heart and appeal directly to the latent sense of wonder and awe and heart-appreciation that God's fantastic love can arouse in human hearts. A capacity for responding is built into every one of us, for "God has dealt to each one a measure of faith" (Romans 12:3).

That "measure" (*metron*, Greek) may be illustrated by my Honda. I bought a "plain-Jane" model and installed the radio myself. Although the radio was not standard equipment, I was pleased to find that the Honda people had built into the car a *metron* or capability for *receiving* the radio. There was an aperture provided for its installation, even holes prepared for the speakers, with wires included. No human being is born with divine love already built in—it must be imported and "installed." But God has built into us the *capacity* for our learning to appreciate it, so we can receive it.

The sowing of such "hearing-of-faith" seed produced early Christians who were not lukewarm. Many sacrificed their all for Him who sacrificed His all for them, singing hymns as they went to martyrdom in the arenas. The true gospel message recovers that Christ-centered motivation. It clearly differentiates between being "under the law" and "under grace" (Romans 6:14, 15).

"Under the Law" Versus "Under Grace"

The usual understanding of "under the law" is "under the condemnation of the law." Although this is true, it is only partly so. When Christ died, He "tasted death for every man," paying the penalty of every man's sin (Hebrews 2:9). In a legal sense therefore He has already taken the condemnation of the law that was due to us. Thus this popular view of "under the law" is reduced to a meaningless phrase. To understand the meaning of being "under the law" we must discover the meaning of its opposite—being "under grace."

If someone risked his life to save you from death, and you understood how horrible that would have been and how much he risked for you, you would ever afterward feel under obligation to him, a gratitude that would motivate you to do anything you could for him. You would not think of *asking him* for a reward; you would want to *give him* one.

To be "under grace" is to be under a new motivation imposed by a "thank You" appreciation of Christ's love for us. "Henceforth" we cannot stop to count the cost of sacrificing for Him, nor can we ask questions about how much or how little He expects of us, or what's the least we can sacrifice in order to get *our* reward.

Our childish questions whether this or that is a "sin that will keep us out of heaven" shrivel up into the pettiness that they are. We forget our striving for reward, for "stars in my crown," and our concern is to help crown *Him* "King of kings and Lord of lords."

Such was the motivation that appealed to the early Christians. "Did the Son of God give Himself for *me*, dying like a criminal on a Roman cross, tasting *my* second death of forsakenness by God? Oh, I must henceforth live for Him!" The result: a beautiful, unmeasured devotion completely devoid of egocentric legalism (cf. 2 Corinthians 5:14, 15; 11:23-30).

To be "under the law" is the simple opposite: to be under a sense of I-ought-to-do-this, or I-should-be-more-faithful, or I-should-sacrifice-more, or I-should-stop-this-bad-habit, or I-should-read-my-Bible-more and pray-more, or I-should-witness-more, etc. The rock-bottom motivation is always a fear of being lost or a hope of reward in heaven, or a search for greater security here and now.

Thus the "under-the-law" motive for healthful living degenerates to a search for longer, happier life for our pleasure here and now rather than to have clearer minds and more healthful bodies with which to serve the One who died for us.

Suppose I meet an alluring temptation to commit adultery. If I say no because of fear of herpes or AIDS, or fear lest the pastor or church board or my friends hear of it, or that my wife will learn of it—I have done the right deed for the wrong reason. This would be an "under-the-law" motivation.

But if I say no as Joseph did in Egypt—"How can I do this great wickedness and sin against God?"—because I can't stand the idea of bringing shame and disgrace on Christ, to add to His pain, I am constrained by a new motivation; I am "under grace."

The Simplicity of Justification by Faith

Is justification by faith only a legal pronouncement that God makes, millions of light years away from us? Does it have no relation to our human hearts? When we make the decision to "accept Christ," do we start the heavenly machinery rolling? Is it then that our name is entered in God's heavenly computer and our eternal social security benefits credited to our account? If so, it would follow that it is our decision which has initiated this process of *legal acquittal*.* An element of pride can enter here; we initiated the process which made our salvation effective! When we get to heaven we can boast that we are there because we made the "decision for Christ."

And this is the last bastion of legalism that seems so difficult for conscientious Christians to recognize. In contrast, the New Testament teaches that the saints are saved because of *Christ's* decision to save them. They simply chose not to *resist* Him!

There can be no pride or "boasting" in true faith. Paul understood how we all share the guilt of "all the world," how "all have sinned," how all of us are involved in the sin of Adam (Romans 3:19, 23). "All *alike* have sinned" (Romans 3:23, NEB). "Death spread to all men, because all sinned" (Romans 5:12). No one of us is innately better than anyone else. As all lions are by nature man-eaters, so all humans are by nature at "enmity against God," and since "whoever hates his brother is a murderer" automatically (Romans 8:7; 1 John 3:15), we are all "*alike*" by nature guilty of the crucifixion of the Son of God. So says Paul. A modern English writer expresses this truth in a penetrating way:

> Fundamentally there is only one sin—rebellion of the human will against the will of God. Insofar as my own will is rebellious, it is in tune with every act of murder, rape, or oppression committed this day in the world. My private acts of selfishness committed today, trivial though they

---

* Justification is a legal term meaning to make right something that was wrong; putting right, making a crooked thing straight, vindicating the right, an acquittal of charges against an individual. The sacrifice of Christ, given once on Calvary's cross, freely gave legal justification to the entire human race. "It follows, then, that as the issue of one misdeed was condemnation for all men, so the issue of one just act is acquittal and life for all men." (Romans 5:18, *The New English Bible*).

Justification by faith is the repentant sinner's believing and appreciating what Christ *has already* accomplished for them; thus it involves a change of heart, it is a heart-reconciliation with God and His righteousness (2 Corinthians 5:14-19).

may seem to me, nevertheless range me on the side of those whose more sensational deeds of cruelty or lust publicly advertise the rebellion of the human will. They bring me into a deep, sympathetic alliance with the murderer, the swindler, and the debauchee. I too, like them, am in rebellion. I too, like them, am serving the self; a little more cautiously and subtly perhaps; being rather more sensitive than they to the earthly cost of extravagance in such matters—but what heed does God pay to that added touch of worldly caution and subtlety? He looks down today upon a human race engaged in obedience or disobedience. There is no third alternative, no discreet maintainings of silence between the praising or blaspheming throngs. In every act we praise or we blaspheme.[1]

But there is also good news in what Paul says that at first thought looks depressing. Just as all have sinned, he continues, so all are "being justified *freely* by His grace." The heavenly machinery is *already* working, long before you make your "decision" to serve the Lord! Since the justification is "free," it must be that everyone has to be included; otherwise it could not be free.

God Himself has taken the initiative—"God set forth [Christ] to be a propitiation by His blood, ... to demonstrate ... His righteousness" (Romans 3:25). And note that it is the "blood" which accomplishes the propitiation.

A propitiation is an offering that changes someone's enmity or alienation into friendship. It doesn't make sense to say that the sacrifice of Christ *propitiates the Father*, because He *already* loved us so much that He *gave* Christ for us. "*God* so loved the world that He gave His only begotten Son." It was *He* who "set forth" Christ on His cross, so that when He is "lifted up ... [He] will draw all peoples" to Himself through the knowledge of that wondrous gift (John 3:16; 12:32).

Nor does it make sense to say that the blood propitiates the devil, or buys him off. He is still our enemy. Who then is propitiated by that blood? Some say that there is a cold legalistic maneuver accomplished—the law was satisfied or that justice was propitiated. But however true this legalistic concept is, the Good News tells of

---

1. H. Blamires (1916-2017), *The Will and the Way* (A Study of Divine Providence and Vocation), pp. 60-63 (1957).

something warm and heart-moving. Law or justice are abstract entities that don't have hearts that can feel. *We* are the ones who have hearts that can feel and need to be reconciled. We are propitiated, moved by the sight of that "blood."

When the sinner stops resisting and lets his proud human heart be melted by that cross, he is reconciled to God and that means he is changed. Now *justification by faith takes place.* This is the process that makes him fully obedient to the law of God. In the past, he was disobedient, and he was selfish. He still has a sinful nature, but now faith *works*, and he does not fulfill those selfish impulses. He crucifies them. He is no longer selfish. There is no thought of reward for himself. Formerly a slave to selfish fear and sin, now he is a slave to Christ's love, and he joins Paul in saying, "The love of Christ constrains us." *This is what it means to be "under grace."* He overcomes "even as" Christ overcame.

The Work That Justification by Faith Accomplishes

(1) *It makes the believer to become obedient to the law of God, not by eradicating his sinful nature but by enabling him to triumph over it.*

The Bible says that God justifies the ungodly (Romans 4:5). It does not mean that He glosses over the sinner's faults, so that he is counted righteous while he is really wicked; but it means that he makes that man a "doer of the law" (Romans 2:23; James 4:11). When God declares an ungodly person righteous, that person becomes obedient. Not merely in an outward way so that his behavior conforms while the inner heart remains wicked. The *heart* is reconciled to God! This is why there can be no higher state than that of justification. It does everything that God can do for a man short of making him immortal, which is done only at the resurrection. Of course, faith and submission to God are exercised continually in order to retain righteousness—in order to remain obedient.

The word of God which speaks righteousness produces righteousness. When the sinner believes and receives that word into his heart by faith, the righteousness of God begins to bear fruit in his life. And since out of the heart are the issues of life, it follows that a new life is thus begun in him; and that life is a life of obedience to the commandments of God. Sanctification is a lifelong process of spiritual

74

growth and maturity, but it never becomes one's "title" to heaven. That "title" remains justification by faith; the "fitness" is sanctification.

(2) *Saving faith is powerful.*

The usual definition of faith is "trust," a self-centered exercise of the will to take hold of an assurance of security. We trust the police because we are afraid to walk the streets without them; we trust the bank because we are afraid to hide our money; we trust the insurance company because we are afraid our house may burn down or our car get wrecked. In each instance, trust rests on an inner fear of personal loss. Is faith in Christ likewise self-centered?

Not New Testament faith. When the apostles wanted to talk about trust, they had Greek words ready to express the idea: *peitho* or *elpizo*. But they never confused faith with self-centered trust.[2] To them faith was a human heart-appreciation of the magnificent love revealed at the cross of Christ (John 3:16; Galatians 5:6, etc). Of course, faith includes an element of trust, but it is only a piece of the pie, not the whole. There is nothing selfish about true faith!

(3) *Genuine justification by faith is meaningless apart from appreciating how close Christ has come to us.*

The early apostles clearly understood how Christ has taken our nature. But in the centuries that have followed, some who opposed the Good News have sought to banish Him far away from us, cutting off His genetic inheritance of our nature. The Roman Catholic dogma of the Immaculate Conception seeks to remove Him from us by declaring that His mother, the Virgin Mary, was "desolidarized" from the human race.[3] (This will be discussed more fully in chapter 10.)

Poor fallen human beings have no strength resting in their flesh to enable them to keep the law of God. And so God imputes to believers the righteousness of Christ, who was made "in the likeness of sinful flesh" so that "the righteousness of the law" might be fulfilled in their lives (Romans 8:3, 4). Christ *took upon* Himself man's nature, and will impute and impart of His own righteousness to those who believe, that is, who appreciate His sacrifice. "Union with Christ" thus becomes more than a mere theological formula.

---

2. The Greek word for faith is *pistis*, and the verb "to have faith" is *pisteuo*.
3. Cf. Fulton Sheen (1895-1979), *The World's First Love*, New York: McGraw-Hill, p. 10 (1952).

New Testament justification by faith gives hope to the hopeless, strength to the weak, life to those who are dead in sin. But does this truth inadvertently fall into the error of the Roman Catholic view which says that justification is meritorious, "making righteous"? The two views are as different as night and day. (A discussion of the contrasts will be found in Appendix B, p. 139).

The everlasting gospel of Revelation 14 breaks through centuries of Catholic and Protestant fog into a clearer view of the sunlit New Testament truth.

How Good News Permeates the Message

A so-called "gospel" without Good News is a counterfeit. The burden of the apostles' message is "glad tidings" (see Acts 13:32-34). This gave people no false assurance of trusting to their personal experience. The burden of their message was how faithful God is, trusting Him (see Romans 8:26-39, for example).

Our problem is our alienation from God due to our guilt and distorted view of His character. Troubles and disappointments arouse bad feelings. Why doesn't He do more to help us? Paul pleaded, "Be reconciled to God," believe the truth about His character, let the blood of Christ wash you clean, and let your enmity be healed and your guilt taken away (2 Corinthians 5:20). Then faith can go to work, producing mighty works of righteousness in the life.

Now it is time to "come boldly to the throne of grace," where we are sure to find grace to help in time of need, because that need is felt by our Savior in the very time of need (see Hebrews 4:14-16). The same temptation that presses you touches Him. His wounds are ever fresh, and He ever lives to make intercession for you.

No matter how much Satan may war against us, assaulting us where the flesh is weakest, we may abide under the shadow of the Almighty, and be filled with the fullness of God's strength.

Why is it that the sun does not slip out of its place? The powerful word of the Savior holds the sun there, and causes it to go on in its course. And *that same power* is to hold up the believer in Jesus.

Thus the gospel emphasis is not on what we must *do* in order to be saved, but on what we must *believe*. And what must we believe? Always, Good News.

There is special power included in forgiveness. We gain very little self-respect in being merely pardoned. If all God does for us is to pardon or excuse our sins, we still must carry the pollution deep within our souls.

But the "blood of the new covenant ... is shed for many for the *remission* of sins." They are to be "blotted out." True forgiveness will do more than pardon us. It will "cleanse us from all unrighteousness" (Matthew 26:28; Acts 2:38; 3:19; 1 John 1:9; 2:1, 2). God's forgiveness is not merely a judicial act by which He sets us free from condemnation. It is not only forgiveness *for* sin, but reclaiming *from* sin.

Most people who have read the following passage have read it backwards, thereby turning the Good News into bad news:

> The flesh lusts [strives] against the Spirit, and the Spirit against the flesh: and these are contrary to one another, so that you do not [cannot, KJV] do the things that you wish (Galatians 5:17).

It is commonly assumed that Paul says you can never really do the *good things* you wish you could do, even with the help of the Spirit. But note that in proper context Paul's meaning is that His power is so much stronger than that of the flesh that you cannot do the *evil things* that your sinful nature prompts you to do.

The previous verse makes the connection clear and teaches fantastic Good News: "I say then: Walk in the Spirit, and *you shall not fulfill the lust of the flesh*." And the following verse further emphasizes the Good News: "Moreover [Greek, *de*, furthermore] if you are led of the Spirit, you are not under the law" (the condemnation of the law).

Still Better News: A People Prepare for Christ's Coming

There is a true aspect of the gospel which has been widely opposed in recent years. The very possibility of a people overcoming all sin so that they might be ready for Christ's coming has been muted and even denied and ridiculed. It has often been denounced as the heresy of "perfectionism."

But the Bible is clear:

> The grace of God that brings salvation has appeared to all men. It teaches us to say "No" to ungodliness and worldly passions, and to live self-controlled, upright and godly lives in this present age, while we wait for the blessed hope—the glorious appearing of our great God and Savior, Jesus Christ,

who gave Himself for us to redeem us from all wickedness and to purify for Himself a people that are His very own, eager to do what is good (Titus 2:11-14, NIV).

Revelation complements this "blessed hope" by describing a people who "follow the Lamb wherever He goes. ... They are blameless" (Revelation 14:4, 5, NIV).

Scripture teaches that those who look "for that blessed hope" will truly, not supposedly, "keep the commandments of God, and the faith of Jesus" (Revelation 14:12). This glorious result will be accomplished through righteousness by faith, not through an *ego*-centered works program.

Tucked away in an obscure text of the Bible is a Good News promise that cannot fail to be fulfilled: "Unto two thousand and three hundred days; then shall the sanctuary be cleansed" (Daniel 8:14, KJV). Amplified and complemented by the message of Hebrews in the New Testament, this prophecy describes the special work of the heavenly High Priest on this cosmic Day of Atonement "in the days of ... the seventh angel, when he shall begin to sound" (Revelation 10:7, KJV; see Hebrews 8, 9, 10). This cleansing of the sanctuary is the work which began in 1844, at the end of that prophetic period of years.

Popular "righteousness by faith" knows nothing of the cleansing of the heavenly sanctuary, nothing of an antitypical Day of Atonement. The idea of a special heart-preparation for the return of Christ is dimly, if at all, comprehended.

The New Testament gospel message sees a successful resolving of the great struggle of the ages between Christ and Satan. The Lord finds a people willing to cooperate fully with Him in these last days. The Good News is that Christ as heavenly High Priest cleanses His sanctuary. It's not *our* job to do it. Our part is to cooperate with Him, *to let Him do it*, and stop *hindering* His Holy Spirit who works continually to lead us away from selfishness and sin and to prepare a people for His soon return.

CHAPTER EIGHT

What Did Christ Accomplish on His Cross?

When Jesus died on the cross, did He make a mere *provision* whereby something *could* be done for us if we first do our part? Or did He actually *do* something for "all men"? We must now look again at that "wondrous cross" and see something that the enemy of our souls wants us to overlook.

Yes, He most certainly did do something for every human soul, more than a mere provision. The Bible often assures us that He "is the propitiation for our sins, and not for ours only but also for the *whole world*" (1 John 2:2). As "all have sinned," so all are "being justified freely by His grace" (Romans 3:23, 24). "God was in Christ reconciling *the world* to Himself, not imputing their trespasses to them" (2 Corinthians 5:19). Jesus came that He "might taste death for *everyone*" (Hebrews 2:9). Through His "righteous act the free gift came to *all men*, resulting in justification of life" (Romans 5:18).

The common idea is that the sacrifice of Christ is only *provisional*, that is, it does nothing for anyone unless he first does something and "accepts Christ." According to this popular idea, Jesus stands back with His divine arms folded, waiting for the sinner to decide to "accept." In other words, salvation is a heavenly process that remains void until *we* take the initiative. Like a washing machine in a Laundromat, it has been *provided*, but it is only provisional. It does nothing for us until we first put in the coins. This sounds reasonable for it superficially explains why many are lost.

In contrast, the gospel which Paul proclaimed shines forth in our texts quoted above: (a) Christ did not limit His sacrifice, for in tasting "death for *everyone*" He died "everyone's" second death, (b) As "all have sinned," so "all" are "being justified freely by His grace." This is a *legal* justification, as we shall soon see. (c) By virtue of Christ's sacrifice, God is not "imputing their trespasses" unto *the world*. He imputed them to Christ instead. This is why no lost person can suffer the second death until after the final judgment, which can come only after the second resurrection (see Revelation 2:10; 20:6-14). And this is why we all can live even now. Our very life is purchased by Him. (d) "The *whole world*" has been redeemed, if only they knew it and believed it and stopped resisting the grace of God.

Every person owes his or her physical life, even this earthly life and all he has or is to the One who "died for *all*." Whether one is a saint or a sinner, if he eats his daily food, he is nourished by the body and the blood of Christ. That means that the cross of Calvary is stamped on every loaf of bread. It is reflected in every water-spring.

When the sinner sees this truth and his heart appreciates its reality, he experiences *justification by faith*. This is therefore far more than a legal declaration of acquittal, for that was made at the cross for "all men." *Justification by faith includes a change of heart.* It is the same as forgiveness. And New Testament forgiveness is more than a mere pardon. The Greek word for forgiveness means a "taking away" of the sin from the heart, reclaiming *from* it (cf. Matthew 1:23 and 26:28).[1]

How Justification by Faith Works

This is how the believer who exercises true faith becomes inwardly and outwardly obedient to all the commandments of God. Christ alone has saved him and justified him, but his faith responds and "works by love." It is a new principle that permeates every nook and cranny of the human heart, "bringing every thought into captivity to Christ … [so that] obedience is fulfilled" (2 Corinthians 10:5, 6).

Such faith, if it is not hindered and adulterated with error, will begin the moment the sinner chooses to respond and will then grow to be so mature and powerful that it will prepare a people for the return of Christ. This is that "everlasting gospel" that we find in Revelation 14:6-14 which is proclaimed to all the world just before the return of Jesus.

Does this mean that all will be saved? No, not all will be saved. But the reason is deeper than that the lost were not clever or prompt

---

1. Jesus says that His blood is shed "for the remission of sins." Remission is more than mere pardon; it is taking the sin away.

enough to seize the initiative. *They will have actually resisted and rejected the salvation already "freely" given them in Christ.* God has taken the initiative to save "all men," but humans have the power, the freedom of will, to thwart and veto what Christ has already accomplished for them and to throw away what was actually placed in their hands.

Nevertheless, there will be some, a "remnant," who do respond wholeheartedly. Christ "shall see the travail of His soul, and be satisfied. By His knowledge My righteous Servant shall justify many" (Revelation 12:17; Isaiah 53:11).

We can cherish our alienation from Him and our hatred of His righteousness until we close the gate of heaven against ourselves. That is sad. But it is not necessary. According to the gospel concept, those who are saved at last are saved due to God's initiative; those who are lost are lost because of their own initiative.

Even the gift of faith is dealt to every man, even as Christ gave Himself to every man (Romans 12:3). What then can prevent every man from being saved? The answer is, Nothing, except the fact that all men will not keep the faith that God gave them. If all would keep it, all would be saved.

It follows that there is not the slightest reason why all who have ever lived should not be saved unto eternal life, except that they would not have it. Christ died for all. So many spurn the gift given so freely.

According to Jesus, the only sin for which anyone can be lost is that of not appreciating and receiving His grace. This is what unbelief is—receiving it in vain. "He who does not believe is condemned . ... And this is the condemnation, that the light has come into the world, and men loved [chose] darkness rather than light" (John 3:17-19).

How can it be that the cross is stamped on every loaf of bread, and even unbelieving sinners enjoy life because of Christ's sacrifice? As the Lamb "slain from the foundation of the world," He has truly "brought life ... to light through the gospel" (Revelation 13:8; 2 Timothy 1:10). The human race was so degraded in the time of the Roman Empire that mankind would have eventually destroyed themselves if Christ had not come when He did in "the fullness of the time" (Galatians 4:4).

Even the wicked today draw their next breath because of Christ's cross, though they do not know the fact. No one can know a moment's joyous laughter except that a price was paid for it by the One on whom was laid "the chastisement for our peace," and by whose "stripes we are healed" (Isaiah 53:5). This is another way of saying that for "all men" He has brought "life," enduring the imputation of their trespasses to Himself, and for those who believe and appreciate His cross, He has also brought "immortality" (2 Timothy 1:10).

Paul rejoices in the grand work that Christ accomplished on His cross: "As through one man's offense judgment came to all men, resulting in condemnation, even so through one Man's righteous act, the free gift came to all men, resulting in justification of life" (Romans 5:18). This is such an astounding statement that people have wrestled with it for centuries. There are four ways that it has been interpreted:

(1) The Calvinist view implies that Paul did not say it quite right—"the free gift ... resulting in justification of life" came only on the elect, not on "all men." Or, the non-elect are so unimportant that they aren't included in "all men." But the text itself denies this view.

(2) The Universalist view understands from this that "all men" must be saved at last. But the Bible often says clearly that in the end some will choose to be lost.

(3) The popular Arminian view also implies that Paul did not say it quite right—"the free gift ... resulting in justification of life" did not actually come upon "all men." Christ only made a *provision* so that it might possibly come *if* but *not until* they do something right first. Unless they activate the heavenly process, nothing happens. The washing machine in the Laundromat is only a provision, for it needs coins. This view is widely believed, for it superficially explains why so many will be lost—they didn't take the initiative to put the coins into the machine. But this view conflicts with what Paul said.

(4) Paul's own view is far better Good News. He said it exactly right: Christ as "the last Adam" has reversed all the evil that the first Adam did. As surely as "all men" were condemned by Adam's sin, so surely "all men" have been *legally* justified by Christ's sacrifice. He has already tasted death for "every man." He is the propitiation for the sins "of the whole world." No one could draw his next breath unless his sins had already been imputed to Christ, for no one, saint or sinner, could bear his own full guilt even for a moment and still live. But human unbelief can negate the justification which has already been given us.

Thus Christ did more than make a mere *provision* for a *possible* salvation that becomes real only *if* we succeed in doing everything just right. As the condemnation came upon all, so the justification comes upon all. *The New English Bible* makes it clear:

> The judicial action, following upon the one offence, issued in a verdict of condemnation, but the act of grace, following upon so many misdeeds, issued in a verdict of acquittal. … It follows, then, that as the issue of one misdeed was condemnation for all men, so the issue of one just act is acquittal and life for all men (Romans 5:16, 18, NEB).

The fact that justification is a free gift is evidence that there is no exception. If it came upon only those who have some special qualification, then it would not be a free gift.

In the light of the cross, therefore, even "neglect" of "so great salvation" is rejection of it. *This is unbelief.* Thus the lost person condemns himself before the universe and unfits himself for eternal life. He shuts himself out of heaven.

The true Good News is far better than we have been led to think. Our salvation does not depend on our cleverness in taking the initiative; it depends on our *believing* that God has taken the initiative in saving us. He elects all to be saved.

The Scandal of God Seeking Man

There is no parable that tells of a lost sheep that must find its way back to the shepherd; but there is one of a Good Shepherd who searches for His lost sheep. The ancient pagans were scandalized by the apostles' teaching that God is not waiting for man to seek Him, but that He is already seeking for man (Luke 15:3-10; 19:10; John 4:23; Romans 10:6-8; 10:10-13). The woman in Christ's parable didn't wait for her lost silver coin to come back; she went looking for it until she found it. The prodigal son came home only because he remembered and was drawn by the father's love. The initiative was always with the father, and the son only responded to it (see Luke 15:4-32).

The Bible teaches that it is not our job to initiate a "relationship" with Christ, for *He* has initiated the relationship with us. Our job is to believe it, to cherish it and to appreciate it.

Neither is it strictly true to say that our salvation depends on our *maintaining* a relationship with the Lord. The Good Shepherd keeps looking for His sheep "*until He find it*" (Luke 15:4). In other words, He wants you to be saved more than you want to be saved. He does not get tired or discouraged as we do because of our unbelief.

Your salvation depends on your believing that He loves you so much that He will maintain that relationship unless you beat Him off. Stop resisting the leading and prompting of the Holy Spirit, who is called "the Comforter." It is He who convicts us of sin and seeks to motivate us to forsake it. He is called to come and sit down beside us and never to leave us (John 14:16-18; 16:7-13). Our devotion is always a *response* to His aggressive, initiating, and on-going love.

In other words, to put the gospel message into very simple words—*salvation depends on faith.* Our job is not to climb up to heaven or descend down to hell looking for Jesus as though He is hiding from us, but to recognize that *He has found* us by "the word of faith, which we preach" (cf. Romans 10:6-8). One would have to be very hard-hearted not to say "Thank You" when he realizes how the Good Shepherd has saved him from the horror of a hell here and now and from the second death at last. Let us not resist or reject His election.

When we ask the Bible question, "What must I do to be saved?" we must let the Bible give the answer. The answer is not, Do this, and do that; get up earlier, work harder at studying and praying; do more witnessing; make more sacrifices; achieve more goals; master more techniques; go to more seminars. The true answer is, "*Believe* on the Lord Jesus Christ, and you will be saved, and your household" (Acts 16:30, 31). The Bible does not teach a heresy. That "believing" is the kind that works and purifies the soul.

The key to our difficulty is understanding what it means to believe. It is folly to permit Satan to preempt that genuine word "faith" through his counterfeits so that we turn away from genuine righteousness by faith and revert to a subtle works program.

People Still Have Problems With the Good News

Doesn't the Bible tell us that it is our job to "seek the Lord"? Do the Old Testament "seek-ye-the-Lord" texts contradict Jesus' New Testament parable of the Good Shepherd seeking us?

It is a mistake to twist Old Testament texts to make them contradict the clear words of Jesus. Jesus came to reveal a "grace [that] did much more abound" (Romans 5:20; 1 Timothy 1:13-16; Titus 3:3-7). We must understand this or we will forever wallow in a subtle form of legalism.

There is nothing in the New Testament that implies that the Savior waits indifferently until the lost sheep somehow seeks his way back. If that were true, wouldn't the sheep have something to boast of? Even the Old Testament texts that *appear* to give that impression do not do so in context.

Look at Isaiah 55:6: "Seek the Lord while He may be found, call upon Him while He is near." That sounds like Isaiah is contradicting Jesus! But take a closer look. The Hebrew word translated "seek" (*darash*) does not primarily mean seek, but "pay attention to," or "inquire of" (cf. its use in 1 Samuel 28:7).[2] Isaiah says, Pay attention to the Lord "while He is near." The prophet emphasizes His nearness, not His farness.

There is no Bible statement that reveals God as indifferently waiting for us to arouse Him from lethargy. Our "seeking" is always represented as a heart-response to His initiative in seeking us. The true gospel gives a beautiful and powerful reason for serving Christ:

> The love of Christ constraineth us; because we thus judge, that if One died for all, then were all dead: and that He died for all, that they which live should not henceforth live unto themselves, but unto Him which died for them, and rose again (2 Corinthians 5:14, 15, KJV).

The apostles proclaimed a message refreshingly different than much that is usually called "gospel" today. The original language implies that those who sense Christ's *agape*-love find it *impossible* "henceforth" to go on living for self. We see the Savior's matchless love, and the sight of Him attracts and subdues our hearts. Alienation and rebellion are healed.

Getting Down to the Roots

The pure gospel provides a deep peace, and it grows in a heart that has been delivered from that subliminal fear that shadows us from our cradle to our grave.

---

2. King Saul asks his servants to "seek" or "find" him "a woman who is a medium." This is the common word that means "seek." It is not *darash*. Next he says, "that I may go to her and inquire of her." That is *darash*, which is translated "seek" in Isaiah 55:6.

Sometimes rage or bitterness erupts from the murky depths of our unknown selves like a volcano we thought was extinct. Molten lava pours forth from deep subterranean emotional fires.

Often they have smoldered from our infancy, yes, perhaps even from conception—like the child who realizes that he or she was the product of lust, of an unwanted pregnancy. Can a fetus share somehow the bitterness of its pregnant mother? After birth the unwanted child can wonder, "Where was God when this happened?" Or the child whose parents did not realize how they were destroying his or her sense of healthy self-respect by fault-finding or pressure to *earn* their love. Many of us carry a crushing load of guilt and alienation which stems from infantile traumas that are in no way our fault. Alcoholism, drug addiction, constitutional depression, sexual degradation, can often find their roots in infancy. Some say that homosexuality is triggered there.

And there are traumas of rejection that can devastate our adult lives, like the death of a spouse, or worse, divorce. Does the gospel have Good News for us?

Yes—justification by faith! It gives you peace with God, as though you had never sinned, and further, *as though no one else had ever sinned against you*. It solves the problem of that deep, deep bitterness that even psychiatrists can't reach. It enables you to forgive others, because you sense their guilt is yours as well "but for the grace of God."

One can even forgive negligent parents or guardians, those who wronged us in childhood, even alcoholic parents.[3] It is practical healing for wounded emotions, always penetrating deeper, and then blending into sanctification. And it is ministered by a High Priest who is "touched with the feeling of our infirmities," our weaknesses (Hebrews 4:15, KJV).

The best modern translation of High Priest is Divine Psychiatrist. He is on duty 24 hours a day; He never takes a holiday from duty; and He is so infinite that He gives you His full attention as if you were the only patient that He has.

---

3. This becomes easier when one remembers that often those who were abused in childhood become child-abusers when they become adults. Guilt is corporate; both child and parent demonstrate it; "the child becomes father to the man."

CHAPTER NINE

Can the Good News Be Too Good?

This is a serious question! Conventional wisdom for thousands of years will tend to say yes. The masses have always considered the Good News to be impossible. This is evident in the fact that they generally take the broad way that leads to destruction and avoid the strait and narrow way (the way of faith) that leads to eternal life (Matthew 7:13, 14).

Jesus makes a fantastic promise, "Go into all the world and preach the gospel to every creature. … And these signs will follow those who believe: In My name they will cast out demons; they will speak with new tongues [languages, Greek]; they will take up serpents; and if they drink anything deadly, it will by no means hurt them; they will lay hands on the sick, and they will recover" (Mark 16:15, 17).

Matthew gives another version of what Jesus said: "All authority has been given to Me in heaven and on earth. Go therefore, and make disciples of all nations. … And lo, I am with you always, even to the end of the age." And John adds what he remembers hearing the Lord say, which is even more astounding: "He who believes in Me, the works that I do he will do also; and greater works than these he will do, because I go to My Father" (Matthew 28:19, 20; John 14:12).

Are these promises too good to be true? The Good News is that they will be fulfilled, without fanaticism and without extremism, in the glorious final message proclaimed by the fourth angel of Revelation 18:1-4. If the Bible is true, the whole world is to be "illuminated" with the glory of a powerful message. It would not be fair for Christ to return unless everyone has had a fair opportunity to hear it and to prepare for His coming. The key to the fulfillment of these promises is in two significant phrases:

(1) A people must "preach the *gospel*," not legalism and not human philosophy; and

(2) The fulfillment will come to him "who believes in Me." "The gospel of Christ … is the power of God to salvation for everyone who *believes*" (Romans 1:16).

"He who believes in Me" means "he who has true faith," the kind that *works* in transforming the life. In other words, there is tremendous power in true righteousness by faith.

God's people must not be impotent in the face of the moral and spiritual plagues that afflict society today. The world faces no end of human disorders now known as addictions—drug abuse, alcoholism, marital infidelity, sexual immorality, corruption, compulsive eating disorders, and widespread psychological depression. A steady and increasing deterioration of the human spirit is bringing millions close to the place where they may be mentally unable even to comprehend the everlasting gospel.

The Bible promises adequate power to cope with these tragic needs. That power is in the gospel. The Holy Spirit has promised to bless with His presence its true proclamation; but if the message is adulterated with legalism or spiritualism so that in any way it is a distortion of the true gospel, to that extent the Holy Spirit's blessing is negated.

Meanwhile the Lord has instructed "four angels" to "hold" the "four winds" of human passion "till we have sealed the servants of our God" (Revelation 7:1-4). The sealing described in Revelation is the final work to be accomplished by the gospel.

The loosing of those "four winds" is a very sad thing, the complete breakdown of social order, decency, morality, fidelity, economic and political security. The Bible says it will be "Babylon" dropping into the sea like a millstone, the end of weddings, Christmases, shopping, sports, materialistic orgies, vacations, sensuality (see Revelation 18). Already we see around us the beginning of this final breakup of order and morality. Psycho-criminal gangs are terrorizing large cities and police are increasingly frustrated in their efforts to maintain even a minimum of security for law-abiding citizens.

Meanwhile, the special message which the three angels of Revelation 14 proclaim is "the everlasting gospel" in the setting of the cosmic Day of Atonement and the cleansing of the heavenly sanctuary. Heaven is concerned about very serious business—getting ready for the end.

The point is simple: if His people will faithfully proclaim that pure gospel message, the Lord has promised that He will do His part to restrain the exploding evil in the world. But if they do not faithfully proclaim the message that alone can prepare a people for the return of Christ, He cannot hold in check those near-exploding global forces of evil. Merely to proclaim a message that prepares people for death is not good enough. That has been done in all past ages. The time must come when there is a message that prepares a people for His second coming.

Surely it was never His will that World Wars I and II should unleash such mayhem and pain in the world, as well as the horrors and violence that are so common in many lands today. The world has been starving for "the everlasting gospel," and still is. It has been said that it is hungry animals that fight.

God's plan is that His people will make a great impact on the world by proclaiming a unique message that Heaven can fully endorse. They must be like little David with five smooth stones facing Goliath, and they will be as successful. The gospel power to prevent those storms of human and national passion is to be in the message itself, not in church institutions, budgets, electronic stimuli, clever advertising, or even organization.

Speaking of power, there are also in the world numerous "faith-healers" and charlatans who prey on people's self-centered motivations. Christ has warned us that in the last days Satan will perfect his clever technique of deception to such an extent that even faithful Christians can be in great danger of being fooled: "False christs and false prophets will arise and show great signs and wonders, so as to deceive, if possible, even the elect" (Matthew 24:24).

Revelation further enlarges on this scenario, describing this power that "performs great signs, so that he even makes fire come down from heaven on the earth in the sight of men. And he deceives those who dwell on the earth by those signs which he was granted to do in the sight of the beast" (Revelation 13:13, 14).

The point that Jesus makes in His warning is that this world power (symbolized as a beast) is not some blatantly non-Christian force such as Communism or satanism. It professes to be Christian, is very popular, and therefore has tremendous potential for deception. And since it brings the last test just before the return of Christ, the stakes are high. It is a *false christ*! There will be no second time around to undo our error if we are deceived the first time.

Now is the time to get ready to meet this test by making certain that we are rooted and grounded in what Paul says is "the truth of the gospel" (Galatians 2:5, 14).

Revelation tells us that the final test will be related to a true understanding of the cross of Christ. "All who dwell on the earth will worship him [the beast], whose names have not been written in the Book of Life of the Lamb slain from the foundation of the world" (Revelation 13:8). The Lamb is a symbol of the crucified Christ.

The false christ will skillfully employ the names and associations of the Christ of the Bible, but his character will be different than that of the One who sacrificed Himself for our redemption. One who truly believes in Christ will appreciate His love (*agape*) to the extent that his own pride will be humbled. Paul says, "I am crucified with Christ" (Galatians 2:20).

The result? The believer in Christ gladly dedicates all to Him, and henceforth delights in obedience to all of God's commandments. He loves the Lord supremely and his neighbor as himself. This experience will be lacking in the "ministry" of the false christ. Pride, love of self, arrogance, and love of the world, will characterize the counterfeit.

Satan can work miracles and even give his followers light and much power, but no sweet love, joy and peace. But there is good news lurking beneath this shadowed truth. The presence of the counterfeit only proves that the genuine is in existence somewhere.

How a Pure Gospel Message Can Have Power

Everywhere the early apostles preached, something happened—either a riot or a revival. The reason they could turn "the world upside down" was not their cleverness or their personalities. The power was in the content of their message.

Peter's sermon at Pentecost reveals the source of their power: they understood what the atonement implies. Not just the Jewish leaders, but all in the Gentile world were declared to be guilty of the rejection and murder of the Son of God. Pentecost was the corporate guilt of all humanity exposed.[1] Enmity against God had blossomed into the supreme crime of eternity. The apostles minced no words in telling it (Acts 2:23-37). It was the proclamation of that truth which catalyzed humanity.

---

1. "Corporate": pertaining to the human race as one "body."

90

The *latter* rain gift of the same Holy Spirit will come before the grain can ripen, as Pentecost was the *early* rain that caused it to germinate. The truth of the gospel will do the work (cf. Galatians 2:14).

Some of the human problems which the gospel of the apostles solved were the same ones that perplex psychiatrists and social scientists today. We have noted the miracles in Corinth that were greater than mere physical healings (see 1 Corinthians 6:9-11). These same problems afflict the human race today, but they have become worse.

These problems are not mere occasional moral lapses. Each becomes a compulsive obsession or addiction, with roots going down to people's toes. Addicts seem powerless to break their slaveries. How were those problems solved in Corinth? Paul gives the answer in his letter to the Corinthians: *by the message of justification by faith.* "You were washed ... , you were sanctified ... , you were justified in the name of the Lord Jesus" (verse 11).

There was frightful moral depravity in the days of the pagan Roman empire. Citizens and slaves were so violently cruel that they reveled in watching human beings fight wild animals and each other to the death. The more blood the more fun. Prostitution was sanctified as a part of religion. But through the proclamation of the gospel, "grace abounded much more," and reigned "through righteousness [by faith] to eternal life" (Romans 5:20, 21). The story of the cross touched secret springs hidden deep in Gentile and Jewish hearts and released latent God-given capabilities undreamed of.

The message placed "under grace" people who were shackled by all kinds of compulsive sin, including that of "abusers of themselves with mankind" (1 Corinthians 6:9, KJV; "homosexuals," NJKV). Now a new compulsion shackled them willingly and gladly to Christ.

The result was a happy one. "Sin shall not have dominion over you," said Paul, "for you are not under law but under grace" (Romans 6:14).

Since 1956 the American Medical Association has said that alcoholism and other addictions are a disease. Proponents of this theory search for hidden biological or hormonal deficiencies in body chemistry, hoping to find a drug that can cure the "disease." Treatment of alcoholism alone costs more than $1 billion a year and is often ineffective. There may well be physiological or chemical factors which become involved in developing addictions, but according to the Bible, the primary initiating cause is a sinful, selfish choice somewhere.

A team of Columbia University psychopharmacologists and psychiatrists reports that a history of depression is a major predictor of addiction. People who have trouble quitting cigarettes generally confirm the relationship between depression and nicotine addiction. Women are more prone to depression than men, says Columbia's Dr. Alexander Glassman, suggesting that depression may lie at the root of addictions. They also have greater difficulty in quitting cigarettes.

Depression is a psychological term that relates to the Biblical term "unbelief." The medicine needed? Something more potent than pharmaceutics: Biblical faith.

What Truth Does a Message of Grace Emphasize?

The apostles' message of grace proclaimed what is often neglected or denied within the church today—the truth of Christ's human nature being *like*, not *unlike*, ours. What impressed those people was the reality of the Son of God coming nigh at hand, taking their nature and being tempted as they were, suffering in their place, accepting their poverty that He might give them His wealth, conquering their temptations by faith but with the same equipment they had. Christ was never depressed, but the Bible assures us that He was *tempted* as we are (Hebrews 4:15). Paul reminded the Corinthians of what they had learned from him: "You know the grace of our Lord Jesus Christ, that though He was rich, yet for your sakes He became poor, that you through His poverty might become rich" (2 Corinthians 8:9).

Here was a power that gripped human hearts as nothing had done in all previous history. Here is how the most hopeless captives found deliverance. The cross-reality burned its way into the deepest recesses of human consciousness as a spiritual catharsis. A new sense of self-respect emerged that nothing could destroy. The pure gospel will do the same work today.

This is why it is not the personalities of the speakers or hierarchical pressures that have such "power." *It is the message itself.* Needless to say, the enemy of Christ opposes such a revelation and would suppress it, and thus keep it from the world. He is determined to make us believe that his clever invention of sin is invincible.

God's Plan for His People

The heart of God yearns for all the heart-burdened captives of Satan in the world today. Christ paid the price for their deliverance, and yet millions, yes billions, are virtually ignorant of His work as High Priest in the heavenly sanctuary. He must depend on His people to proclaim and to demonstrate that unique message so as to deliver from Satan's grip. He has promised that they are to be the avenue through which His much more abounding grace is to be communicated to the world. This is a grace greater than is understood by those who have no knowledge of the special ministry of Christ in cleansing the sanctuary:

> It shall come to pass afterward [in the last days] that I will pour out My Spirit on all flesh. ... And it shall come to pass that whoever calls on the name of the Lord shall be saved. For in Mount Zion and in Jerusalem there shall be deliverance, as the Lord has said, among the remnant whom the Lord calls (Joel 2:28, 32; Acts 2:17).

> The earth will be filled with the knowledge of the glory of the Lord, as the waters cover the sea (Habakkuk 2:14).

> We do not have a High Priest who cannot sympathize with our weaknesses, but was in all points tempted as we are, yet without sin. Let us therefore come boldly to the throne of grace, that we may obtain mercy and find grace to help in time of need (Hebrews 4:15, 16).

> The angel swore by Him who lives forever ... that ... in the days of the sounding of the seventh angel, when he is about to sound, the mystery of God would be finished, as He declared to His servants the prophets. ... Then the seventh angel sounded: ... Your wrath has come, and the time of the dead, that they should be judged. ... Then the temple of God was opened in heaven, and the ark of His covenant was seen in His temple (Revelation 10:6, 7; 11:15, 18, 19).[2]

> I saw another angel coming down from heaven, having great authority, and the earth was illuminated with his glory.

---

2. "The ark of His covenant" identifies the second apartment of the Heavenly Sanctuary where Christ ministers in the antitypical Day of Atonement.

... And I heard another voice from heaven saying, "Come out of her [Babylon], my people, lest you share in her sins, and lest you receive of her plagues" (Revelation 18:1, 4).

Note that word, "having great *authority*." In the original language it is the same word that Jesus used when He told His disciples that "all authority has been given to Me in heaven and on earth" (Matthew 28:18). Now, in this time of His closing work of atonement, He is finally able to communicate that "authority" through His people on earth so that in His name they will be empowered to do the "greater works" than He did on earth. The world is to be "illuminated with His glory" through a clear, unadulterated, uncorrupted proclamation of His Good News, not by impressing them with physical miracles.

The pure, true gospel of the grace of God had such power on Paul that he found it impossible to go on living for self. It made him a "new creation." To be reconciled to God, to have the invisible barrier removed that had beclouded his soul all his life, was totally joyous. The cross captured him forever, and he begs us not to look at it and yawn in boredom: "We then, as workers together with Him also plead with you not to receive the grace of God in vain" (2 Corinthians 5:14-6:1).

The unique message of righteousness by faith that the Lord sends begins to reproduce in modern human hearts the same selfless devotion that motivated Paul long ago.

Let us immerse ourselves in Paul's message of grace so that we can feel those gospel waves rolling over us:

> For the promise that he would be the heir of the world was not to Abraham or to his seed through the law, but through the righteousness of faith. ... It is of faith that it might be according to grace, so that the promise might be sure to all ... those who are of the faith of Abraham, who is the father of us all. (Romans 4:13, 16).

> Through our Lord Jesus Christ ... we have access by faith into this grace in which we stand. ... The grace of God and the gift by the grace of the one Man, Jesus Christ, abounded to many. ... Those who receive abundance of grace and of the gift of righteousness will reign in life through the One, Jesus Christ. ... Where sin abounded, grace abounded much more, so that as sin reigned in death, even so grace might reign through

righteousness to eternal life through Jesus Christ our Lord (Romans 5:1, 2, 15, 17, 20, 21).

Shall we continue in sin that grace may abound? Certainly not! How shall we who died to sin live any longer in it? (Romans 6:1, 2).

Sin shall not have dominion over you, for you are ... under grace (Romans 6:14).

We must not try to rewrite Paul and force him to teach the helpless legalism of try-harder-to-be-good, try-not-to-sin. Astounding as it may seem to us today, he is saying that the power of sin is broken by grace. Note what is implicit in this passage:

(1) Righteousness by faith is not cold theology. It is the ministry of grace.

(2) Faith provides access into this grace, that is, a heart appreciation of the love of God opens the gates of access to hope and glory. Here is plenty of reason for self-respect.

(3) "The gift by the grace ... abounded to many." All who choose to breathe this life-giving atmosphere of grace will live, and grow up to the stature of men and women in Christ Jesus.

(4) Grace is greater than our sin. (That is stupendous!)

(5) Believed and received, grace reigns in the life like a king.

(6) Grace abounding makes it *impossible* for the believer to continue living in sin. Obsessions, captivity to evil habits, alienations, are disarmed.

(7) Grace thus imposes a new captivity which is an unending motivation to holiness of life.

How Can You Be Sure That You Are Included in This Grace?

Not one human soul in all the world is left out. See how the ministry of grace reaches every human soul:

The grace of God that brings salvation has appeared to all men. It teaches us to say "No" to ungodliness and worldly passions, and to live self-controlled, upright and godly lives in this present age, while we wait for the blessed hope—the

95

glorious appearing of our great God and Savior, Jesus Christ, who gave Himself for us to redeem us from all wickedness and to purify for Himself a people that are His very own, eager to do what is good (Titus 2:11-14, NIV).

To each one of us grace was given according to the measure of Christ's gift (Ephesians 4:7).

Let us examine these jewels:

(1) The Holy Spirit imparts to "all men" an intruding sense of the kindness and mercy of God, knocking for entrance to all despairing, depressed, worldly hearts, and also to hearts that are arrogant and self-sufficient. Their time of depression is also sure to come—perhaps when healing will be too late. Listen, look, don't slam the door shut, pause to appreciate that grace, and you will find yourself beginning to cherish it.

(2) In this passage there is an insight that the Supreme Court needs to see. Much as we may excuse ourselves by thinking that addictions to alcohol, drugs, or lust are merely a "disease," they are in reality *volitional*. The problem is that the human will is held captive. But there is Good News: the grace of Christ actually teaches us how to exercise a *controlling* volition, how to "say no" to impulses to evil. Again, it is understanding the cross that makes this little-understood power become reality.

No addict in all the world faces a more terrible compulsion than Jesus felt as He knelt in Gethsemane and prayed, "O My Father, if it is possible, let this cup pass from Me; nevertheless, not as I will, but as You will" (Matthew 26:39). And a few hours later, the compulsive temptation to come down from the cross and abandon His suffering was even stronger. No one has ever felt such tugging at the soul. No sinful patterns of response to temptation that we have acquired even through a lifetime of repeated failures can be stronger than the Savior's power of salvation.

(3) When the grace of God teaches us also to say what Jesus said to temptation—No—this is not a vain choice. When grace teaches us to say that powerful word, the result is guaranteed: we henceforth "live self-controlled, upright and godly lives in this present age," even with alluring sensual temptations all around us. It would be no great achievement to live such lives in perfect surroundings, but Paul

adds that God's great salvation is demonstrated in a wicked world, as wicked as the one that crucified the Son of God.

(4) This deliverance by grace fills the heart with "the blessed hope" of seeing Jesus face to face at His return. Paul's righteousness by faith is linked to the hope of Christ's return, and the message which prepares for His return is the message of the grace of Christ.

(5) Thus the secret of this marvelous power is in that sacrifice where "He gave Himself for us." This penetrates deeper than all the psychiatry in the world in probing to the source of our sin and alienation. The believer actually achieves union with Christ.

(6) The Savior does a good job when He saves; no lingering root of "wickedness" is left in the heart to produce a future fall from grace. He is like a skillful surgeon who removes all of the cancer. Hear this plea from a writer who understood at least the beginning of that abounding grace:

> Do you want to be like Jesus? Then receive the grace that He has so fully and so freely given. Receive it in the measure in which *He has given it*, not in the measure in which you think you deserve it. Yield yourself to it, that it may work in you and for you the wondrous purpose for which it is given, and it will do it. It will make you like Jesus.[3]
>
> Salvation from sin certainly depends upon there being more power in grace than there is in sin. … Wherever the power of grace can have control, it will be just as easy to do right as without this it is easy to do wrong.
>
> No man ever yet naturally found it difficult to do wrong … because man naturally is enslaved to a power—the power of sin—that is absolute in its reign. … But let a mightier power than that have sway, then … it will be just as easy to serve the will of the mightier power.
>
> But grace is not simply more powerful than sin. … There is much more power in grace than there is in sin. … Just so much more hope and good cheer there are for every sinner in the world.[4]

Is this too good to be true? Beware lest you let yourself think so, for it is dangerous to doubt how good the Good News is.

---

3. Alonzo T. Jones, *Review and Herald*, April 17, 1894.
4. Ibid., September 1, 1896.

CHAPTER TEN

The Precious Nearness
of Our Savior

When Peter foolishly tried to walk on the water and began to sink, he cried out, "Lord, save me" (Matthew 14:30). It's terrible to know you are about to drown, but it's comforting then to know that a lifeguard is very near to save you.

We are all Peter sinking in the seas of addiction and selfishness, and we all need a Savior who is near at hand and not afar off. We know only too well how strong is the undertow that sucks us into the maelstrom, and how dark are those depths. We just do not have the strength to save ourselves.

Evil passions, hatreds, and lusts, lurk beneath the surface in all our hearts awaiting a provocation sufficient to arouse them. We don't want to say or do things that we later regret, but before we know it we are embroiled again, and deeper guilt poisons our happiness. Habits of appetite, drugs, tobacco, alcohol, illicit loves, infatuations, mock us as unconquerable.

These feelings, resentments, hatreds, and lusts roll over us like ocean waves. Deep emotions that the commandment forbids when it says, "You shall not covet," are the uncontrollable urges that caused the self-righteous Saul of Tarsus at last to recognize the haunting reality of sin in his heart (Romans 7:7-11).[1]

Youth (and many adults) with raging hormones face problems with illicit sex. The devil rejoices to boast that Christianity hasn't helped much, and the Islamic world in particular consider this as evidence of moral depravity built-in as an intrinsic part of Christianity. A

---

1. What probably enlightened Paul as to his true heart need for a Savior was the commandment, "You shall not covet ... your neighbor's wife" (Exodus 20:17).

1980s survey of 1,006 American girls concludes: "Religion-conscious girls are 86 percent more likely to say it's important to be a virgin at marriage than non-religion-conscious girls. However, *religion-conscious girls are only 14 percent more likely to be virgins than the non-religion-conscious girls.*" [2]

Each year more than a million American teenage girls become pregnant. If present trends continue, 40 percent of today's 14-year-olds will be pregnant at least twice before age 20.[3] Former U. S. Surgeon General C. Everett Koop said that 70 percent of American adolescents are sexually active—that is, practicing fornication. "If you tell that 70 percent to just say no, they laugh. And if they try to say no, they find it very difficult."

Such lack of self-control before marriage usually programs these youth to future marital infidelity. Jesus' words have been fulfilled all around us, "Because lawlessness will abound, the love [*agape*] of many will grow cold" (Matthew 24:12). As surely as night follows day, the loss of *agape* initiates the infidelity-crime-violence-poverty syndrome.

This is the dark world we live in. Multitudes suffer in despair, as Paul did, for they don't really want to slide down into moral suicide. They don't know how to handle peer pressure and those compulsive hormonal urgings.

Paul touched everyone's raw nerve when he complained of himself, "I do not understand what I do; for I don't do what I would like to do, but instead I do what I hate. ... Even though the desire to do good is in me, I am not able to do it. I don't do the good I want to do; instead, I do the evil that I do not want to do.... Evil is the only choice I have. ... Sin ... is at work in my body. What an unhappy man I am! Who will rescue me from this body that is taking me to death?" (Romans 7:18-24, GNB).

Whether this is the converted or unconverted Paul is beside the point. Paul uses the corporate *ego*, referring to humanity in general "in Adam." Here is universal mankind crying out for help. And help is much closer than we have thought.

Paul answers his despairing question himself:

2. Leslie Jane Nonkin, *I Wish My Parents Understood*, NY: Penguin; emphasis supplied.
3. *Time* magazine, December 9, 1985.

What the law could not do in that it was weak through the flesh, God did by sending His own Son in the likeness of sinful flesh, on account of sin: He condemned sin in the flesh (Romans 8:3).

This is the Savior who has come *very near*. But the problem is that the scandal of nearly two thousand years of apostate Christianity has removed that Savior far off from us. If it were not for this terrible falsehood that has put Him far away, it would be impossible for Christian youth to say things like, "I have a lot of work to do if I want to be saved," or "I wish I could be completely good, but it's not always easy," or "I want to serve God, but I find it very hard" (see statements in chapter 3).

The *Chicago Tribune* reported that a Gallup poll found that an upsurge in America's religious interest was cancelled with a similar swing toward immoral behavior. "There is no doubt that religion is growing," Gallup conceded. "But we find that there is very little difference in ethical behavior between church-goers and those who are not active religiously. ... Levels of lying, cheating, and stealing are remarkably similar in both groups."[4]

Can't you hear Satan's hosts cheering "Whoopee!" at news like that? When Jesus made His debut into the world, the angelic fanfare announced, "He will save His people *from* their sins" (Matthew 1:21). Why doesn't the world get to see some clear evidence that His people are indeed saved *from*, not *in* their sins? What has happened?

The reason is that "the little horn" power, "Babylon," has "cast truth down to the ground" and developed a "transgression of desolation" (Daniel 8:12, 13). It has hidden Christ from clear view while professing to worship Him, and substituted a far-away "Christ" who cannot save from sin but can only condone our living in sin. A massive cloud of confusion has enveloped the true Christ, like clouds that hide a mountain peak, so that Christianity is rendered virtually impotent to make the world a better place to live in. And billions do not know the clever switch that has happened.

The New Testament gospel message discloses the nearness of the Savior, and how powerfully He can deliver from the tentacles of deep,

---

4. Quoted in *Passing the Torch*, by Roger Dudley, *Review and Herald*, p. 39 (1986).

deep sin. It is a message that the world is literally dying to hear. Let us examine it more closely.

The Savior Who Came All the Way to Where We Are

Youth in particular are overjoyed with the New Testament message that presents Christ as taking upon Himself our fallen nature, facing our temptations, feeling their full strength, knowing how we feel, and yet gaining the complete victory in sinless character and sinless living. It is as though they turn a corner and come unexpectedly face to face with Jesus Himself. The experience expressed in Isaac Watts' hymn comes alive for these youth:

> Forbid it Lord, that I should boast
> Save in the death of Christ my God;
> All the vain things that charm me most,
> I sacrifice them to His blood.

For thousands of years paganism has represented God as being far away. When the Roman Empire changed its official religion midstream in its history, a corrupt form of Christianity replaced its paganism. But it incorporated the same dark idea of God being far away, separated from humanity. The fundamental idea of the papacy is that God is so holy that He would never come so near to us as to take our flesh and conquer sin where it has taken root in our sinful, depraved nature.

For this reason, Roman Catholicism has developed the "dogma" of the Immaculate Conception. The Virgin Mary, the mother of Jesus, must be cut off from inheriting the genetic nature of humanity, so that she can give to her Son a different kind of humanity than we have. He must be "exempt" from having to face the problems we must face.

This teaching logically maintains that sin in human nature is invincible—in other words, it is impossible not to sin if one has normal human nature. The idea is that sin and human nature belong together. Millions accept this without realizing that it concedes that Satan has been right all along in his rebellion against God (see Job 1 and 2).

The reason is this: Satan claims that his invention of sin proves that God is wrong in requiring obedience to His holy law. Obedience is impossible for fallen mankind, Satan claims; and if Christ had become truly man by taking our fallen, sinful nature, He would have been forced to sin just as we assume that we are forced to sin. He could not have resisted, and neither can we resist.

This idea requires that sin somehow resides in the genes and chromosomes, and therefore Christ must be "exempt" from taking our genes and chromosomes, our genetic inheritance. He must not come "in the likeness of sinful flesh," but must be kept away as far as possible from sinful flesh.

A profound element of deception is implicit in this view. Ostensibly it *appears* to be Christian in that it seems to glorify Christ's sinlessness, and for sure He was sinless; but in reality this dogma separates Him from humanity, and thus denies His true victory over sin in righteousness. It is a skillful subterfuge in that it cuts Him off from partaking of our true human nature and is thus a fulfillment of the apostle John's warning against "the spirit of the Antichrist":

> Every spirit that confesses that Jesus Christ has come in the flesh is of God, and every spirit that does not confess that Jesus Christ has come in the flesh is not of God. And this is the spirit of the Antichrist (1 John 4:2, 3).

The Greek word for "flesh" is *sarx*, which always means the sinful, fallen flesh (or nature) which all human beings share alike. The Bible knows of no other kind of "flesh," and John knows of no "exemption" which separates Christ from taking our flesh. The former Roman Catholic TV evangelist Fulton Sheen makes the point very clear:

> The word "immaculate" is taken from two Latin words meaning "not stained." "Conception" means that, at the first moment of her conception, the Blessed Mother in the womb of her mother, St. Anne, ... was preserved free from the stains of original sin. ... Mary was desolidarized and separated from that sin-laden humanity ... at the moment of her conception ... [This was a] special privilege accorded to Mary. ... She is unique, ... shown a special favor, ... the new Eve, ... humanly perfect! There ought to be an infinite separation between God and sin. ... [He] lifted up one woman by preserving her from sin, ... *someone who would mediate between us and Christ as He mediates between us and the Father.*[5]

---

5. Fulton Sheen, *The World's First Love*, McGraw-Hill, pp. 10-12 (1952); emphasis original.

Mary was chosen by God ... by being preserved free from the primal sin that had infected all humanity. ... In Mary, there was hardly any earth at all except herself; all was Heaven. ... She alone was of earth, and yet she, too, seemed more of Heaven.[6]

No great triumphant leader makes his entrance into the city over dust-covered roads, when he could come on a flower-strewn avenue. Had Infinite Purity chosen any other port of entrance into humanity but that of human purity, it would have created a tremendous difficulty—namely, how could He be sinless, if He was born of sin-laden humanity? If a brush dipped in black becomes black, and if cloth takes on the color of the dye, would not He ... have also partaken of the guilt in which all humanity shared? If He came to this earth through the wheatfield of moral weakness, He certainly would have some chaff hanging on the garment of His human nature.[7]

This is a dogma that has no support in Scripture. It twists the Good News of a victorious Savior who saves *from* sin into the defeatist bad news that says sin is too strong for even Christ to defeat in the flesh. What a clever vindication of Satan's point of contention! Since we are all "sin-laden humanity" living our lives in "the wheatfield of moral weakness," we can never get rid of that "chaff" until we go to a place called purgatory. If Jesus had been truly tempted as we are, He would have sinned; and the corollary is that it is equally impossible for us not to sin.

The Bible gives us better news than that. After he described his despair in Romans 7, Paul found joyful hope in the Good News of a Savior who came all the way to where we are, that He might save us *from our sins*. "There is therefore now no condemnation to those who are in Christ Jesus. ... For the law of the Spirit of life in Christ Jesus has made me free from the law of sin and death" (Romans 8:1, 2). What does this mean? How deep and thorough is Christ's deliverance from our compulsive habits of sin?

---

6. Ibid., pp. 22, 26.
7. Ibid., pp. 61, 62.

"No condemnation" means release from our inner sense of divine judgment which has hung over us all our lives. Although these feelings of psychic wrong and maladjustment are deep and penetrating, "the law of the Spirit of life in Christ Jesus" is even deeper and more far-reaching. A new principle delivers us from tentacles of fear, guilt, and moral disorder that have enslaved our souls, even from our infancy.

No psychiatrist can accomplish such a profound catharsis of the human soul as can this "law of the Spirit of life in Christ Jesus." Wrongs and anxieties that even our parents could not relieve find inner healing. "When my father and my mother forsake me [where they leave off], then the LORD will take me up," says David (Psalm 27:10). He who believes the true gospel enjoys the new birth, which is a power working in him for righteousness as much stronger than the power of inherited tendencies to evil as our heavenly Father is greater than our earthly parents.

A glorious reality is disclosed in Paul's presentation of our nigh-at-hand Christ. The reason why Christ has come so close to us is revealed here:

> What the law could not do in that it was weak through the flesh, God did by sending His own Son in the likeness of sinful flesh, on account of sin: He condemned sin in the flesh, *that the righteous requirement of the law might be fulfilled in us* who do not walk according to the flesh but according to the Spirit (Romans 8:3, 4).

The word "likeness" in the Greek means *identical, the same as*. It cannot mean *unlike* or *different from*. Christ who is fully God now became fully man, not "desolidarized" from the human race. He built a divine-human bridge that spanned the gulf of alienation that sin has made, with foundations that reach all the way to the deepest root within the nature of the most helplessly lost sinner on earth.

In no way did He side-step reality by the deceit of an "exemption" from what we must battle with. Such a contrived exemption would negate the basic principle of righteousness by faith and contradict all of Scripture. Further, it would cast Christ in the role of a deceiver pretending to conquer sin when He never even came close enough to fight the battle where sin is. Paul's intent is to present Christ as perfectly equipped to solve the problem of sin where it is—deep within our fallen nature. Here is the bastion where the dragon has made his last stand, and here is where Christ confronts him. Yet Christ remained perfectly sinless.

A fierce battle is being fought between Christ and Satan over this issue. There is no problem with sin being conquered in sinless nature, different from our sinful flesh. That battle was won long ago in heaven when two-thirds of the angels overcame Satan's temptations in sinless nature (Revelation 12:7-17). For Christ to come to earth to fight that same battle over again would be redundant. You don't win World War II by re-fighting the War of 1812. The battle now is with sin having taken root in sinful human nature, in sinful flesh.

Satan arrogantly claims that his invention of sin has matured in human nature to the place where it now proves God is wrong. It cannot be overcome! And most Christians implicitly agree with Satan. They excuse their continued sinning by saying, "I'm only human! The devil makes me do it." Here is the slimy trail of the great serpent. This is the main reason why the Gallup poll is forced to record so little difference in moral and ethical behavior between Christians and non-Christians.

This false doctrine is enslaving the world with wretched misery. But the true Christ slew the dragon in his last lair, proved that human sin is willful. He created in mankind who believe, a new abhorrence of sin that will lead to its final eradication. Thus He set the captive will of sinful man free to say no to sin, and to "fulfill all righteousness" (cf. Matthew 3:15).

The Reason Why Christ Can Save Every Sinner on Earth

The gospel message is focused like a spotlight in the Book of Hebrews. Here we see how Christ's closeness qualifies Him to penetrate to these inner recesses of our psychic, sinful alienation:

> We see Jesus, who was made a little lower than the angels ... that He, by the grace of God, might taste death for everyone. For it was fitting for Him ... to make the author of their salvation perfect through sufferings. For both He who sanctifies, and those who are being sanctified are all of one, for which reason He is not ashamed to call them brethren. ...
>
> Inasmuch then as the children have partaken of flesh and blood. He Himself likewise shared in the same, that through death He might destroy Him who had the power of death,

that is, the devil, and release those who through fear of death were all their lifetime subject to bondage (Hebrews 2:9-15).

For verily He took not on Him the nature of angels; but He took on Him the seed [*sperm*] of Abraham (verse 16, KJV).

Therefore, in all things He had to be made like His brethren, that He might be a merciful and faithful High Priest in things pertaining to God, to make propitiation for the sins of the people. For in that He Himself has suffered, being tempted, He is able to aid those who are tempted (verses 17, 18).

Let us examine the spiritual riches in this treasure-chest of truth:

(1) Christ has tasted our second death, the ultimate horror of deepest despair beyond even the threshold of our emotional undoing.

(2) He was made perfect through His sufferings.

(3) He is "one" with us.

(4) He calls us "brethren," that is, He is closer to us than family members to one another. He is not cut off or "exempt" from "blood" relationship to us.

(5) Although He was always God in human flesh, He laid aside the advantages of His divinity so that He had to learn to trust in God as we must learn to trust.

(6) He "took part" of the "flesh and blood" of the descendants of fallen Adam, *not that of the sinless Adam*. That "flesh and blood" had to include the hormonal temptations which we experience. Yet He did not sin. (Temptation itself is not sin; the sin lies in yielding to it.) There was no sin in Him.

(7) Specifically, He did not take the nature of sinless beings, but that of the "seed," the genetic *descendants of Abraham*. Thus, in the strongest language possible we are assured that Christ *took upon* His sinless nature our sinful nature, *that He might know how "to aid those who are tempted"* (verse 18).

(8) With no exemption, He was "made like" unto us.

(9) Thus He has become a "merciful and faithful High Priest," our divine-human Physician and Psychiatrist of our souls. His perfect sinlessness qualifies Him.

(10) In every way that we are tempted, because of His utter sinlessness, His victory over sin, He is able to help us.

How Was Christ Tempted?

Did Mary give Him our true human nature, or was the inheritance of our true humanity denied to Him? Was He "desolidarized" from us? [8]

Hebrews reiterates the answer: "We do not have a High Priest who cannot sympathize with our weaknesses, but was in all points tempted as *we* are, yet without sin" (Hebrews 4:14-16). Paul says He "was born of the seed [genetic inheritance] of David according to the flesh" (Romans 1:3). He took our nature, yet He did not sin, so that He might save us from the sin which is in our nature.

Jesus Himself tells us how He had to deny His "own will" in order to follow His "Father's will." Thus His life on earth was a constant struggle against the identical temptations to indulge self that we feel (John 5:30; 6:38; Matthew 26:39; Romans 15:3). We have yielded to self and therefore we are sinners. He constantly denied self. Thus He was sinless. He was never selfish, even for a moment. And His unselfishness cost Him the death of the cross.

This is tremendous Good News! No matter how deep or how strong your temptation may be to give in to self, Christ was tempted that same way, "yet without sin." And that's not all! A powerful "therefore" follows Hebrews 4:15: "Let us therefore come boldly ... and find grace to help in time of need." His "likeness of sinful flesh" gave Him perfect entrance to condemn that very sin that enslaves you and me—judge it, pronounce sentence on it, kill it.

We are invited to be "bold" in Him and not to hang back timidly as though we are doomed to defeat.

The Strange Opposition to the Nearness of the Savior

Some tell us that Christ could not have been tempted as we are, for there were no TVs in His day, no ice cream parlors, no vodka, no sport cars, etc. But that superficial judgment fails to appreciate

---

8. The word was coined by Fulton Sheen in his defense of the Roman Catholic dogma of the Immaculate Conception. Two wires that are soldered together are inseparably joined. To "desolidarize," in the Catholic idea, is to separate forever.

that every temptation to sin that we can experience is directed at our primal love of self; and He knows every avenue of that sin's appeal. Knowing how strong the temptation is, He sympathizes with us, but even that is not all. Mere sympathy and pity would not help us. His full-time job is *saving* us from *yielding* to those temptations. We "come boldly," not timidly, in a prayer of faith to obtain that help.

Note the clear insistence that although Christ came close to us, taking our sinful nature, He was "yet without sin." Not even by a thought or word would He yield to the tempter. "The prince of this world cometh, and hath nothing in Me," He said (John 14:30, KJV). He always remained "that holy One" (Luke 1:35). The struggle against sinful temptation was so fierce and so dangerous that He sweat drops of blood in His agony (Hebrews 5:7; 12:3, 4), a more terrible ordeal than any of us have known.

The struggle to yield your will to be "crucified with Him" may be painful, but it is easier than your being crucified alone. And living the life of resultant resurrection "with Him" is easier than wearing yourself out in continuing to fight *against* the Holy Spirit.

A Magnificent Promise Especially for These Last Days

The Lord has something special for His people living in the very end of time: "To him who overcomes I will grant to sit with Me on My throne, as I also overcame and sat down with My Father on His throne" (Revelation 3:21). He ministers this special privilege now when sin and temptation seem stronger and more alluring than ever before and when we humans are still weaker and more susceptible to falling.

In these last days, the fact of the Savior taking our fallen, sinful flesh, becomes a more precious truth than ever before. His overcoming is not only an example to us. (An example is useless if you don't know how to follow it!) Our Example becomes our training-Exemplar. He identifies with you and you identify with Him. Your temptation becomes His temptation; and your failure becomes His concern. Your success is His victory, for you are joined in a yoke with Him, and He does the pulling of the heavy weight. Our job is to stay with Him and to cooperate with Him, yielding our will to Him. Don't ever leave the happy yoke that binds you to Him (Matthew 11:28-30). That's the best place to be, forever.

Christ knew that in these last days Satan would lead multitudes of human beings into drug addiction, alcoholism, crime, lust, child abuse, homosexuality, pornography, fornication, adultery, bulimia—all temptations that seem irresistible because we have a sinful nature. The lost sheep has strayed further from the fold than ever before, but the Good Shepherd goes further than ever before "until He find it." This means that as a divine Psychiatrist He probes ever more deeply into the why of our last-day weaknesses, and provides full healing. Sin abounding means that there is grace much more abounding.

Paul frequently speaks of "the righteousness" of Christ (cf. Romans 3:21-26; 5:18). This significant phrase implicitly requires the understanding that in His incarnation Christ took the fallen, sinful nature of man. The reason is obvious.

"Righteousness" is a word that is never used of beings with a sinless nature. We read of "holy" angels or unfallen angels, but never of *righteous* angels. Adam and Eve before the fall were innocent and holy, but never do we read that they were *righteous*. They could have *developed* a righteous character if they had resisted temptation, but righteousness has become a term that means holiness that has confronted temptation in sinful human nature and has perfectly overcome. And that is what Christ as the true God-man has done.

The word means justification, and something that is sinless can not need justification. The innate meaning of the word is straightening something that is crooked, correcting something that is unjust.

One who has only a sinless nature would be holy, but could not be said to be righteous. Christ was sinless, but He "took" our sinful, crooked nature and in it lived a perfect life of holiness. This gives Him title to that glorious name, "THE LORD OUR RIGHTEOUSNESS" (Jeremiah 23:6).

Therefore Jude says He "is able to keep you from stumbling, and to present you faultless before the presence of His glory with exceeding joy." Revelation corroborates this promise by displaying a people who stand "without fault before the throne of God." Thus He can say of His people, "The marriage of the Lamb has come, and His wife has made herself ready" (Jude 24; Revelation 12:17; 14:5, 12; 19:7, 8).

The secret of their overcoming is not a special works program of trying harder than ever before. It is the recovery of a purer *faith* than any former generation have attained, a previously unrealized intimacy of sympathy with Christ, a heart-appreciation of Him, a "surveying" of His cross with all the melting of frozen hearts that follows. Nothing else but that contrite concern for the honor of Christ can "keep you from falling." Selfish concern, fear of hell, working for reward in heaven, will fail.

The Third Angel's Message and the Cleansing of the Sanctuary

Our addiction to sin stems from a sense of alienation from God and from one another. A profound loneliness follows. How has Christ abolished this darkness? The Bible reveals how those who were "aliens, ... having no hope and without God in the world ... have been made near by the blood of Christ." He has "abolished *in His flesh* the enmity, ... that He might reconcile them ... to God ... through the cross, thereby putting to death the enmity" (Ephesians 2:12-17).

Many go on year after year "having no hope, and without God in the world." But this alienation was endured by the tempted Jesus as He hung on the cross in His last hours. No one has ever felt so bereft of hope and joy as He when He cried out, "My God, My God, why have You forsaken Me?" (Matthew 27:46).

It was in that final hour of total darkness of soul that Jesus drank our bitter cup to its dregs. That was when He tasted real "death for every man" (Hebrews 2:9). Do you feel as though the heavens were brass above you, the earth as iron beneath, that no one cares, that Heaven seems to have slammed the door against you, that nothing lies before you but darkness? *That is precisely how Jesus felt*, for that is the essence of "the second death." He "tasted" it so that you might not have to feel that way. You can thank Him for enduring that cross for you.

In His closing ministry on this great Day of Atonement He is working hard night and day to complete that reconciliation in the hearts of all who by faith sympathize with Him in that special work.

We can find the most intimate portrayals of Christ's humiliation and excruciating personal pain and victory in what seems an unlikely place—in the Psalms. There it is revealed that Christ took our place, and had the nature of the whole human race. And in Him meet all the weaknesses of mankind, so that every man on the earth who can be tempted finds in Him power against that temptation. For every soul there is in Jesus Christ victory against it all. Psalms 22 and 69 are His cries of woe as He hung on His cross.

In that dark hour when He suffered alone, He built that glorious bridge over the chasm of alienation that sin has caused. His magnificent achievement is called "the atonement," the making at-one of those who were separated—you and God.

That alienation, unrelieved by a knowledge of the gospel, is the fundamental reason why so many youth seek illicit physical intimacies, now more than ever before. Their souls are hungry and empty for the reality which atonement with Christ alone can fill. Frightening them with warnings of pregnancy, VD, AIDS, abortion, or hell, does nothing solid to help them resist temptation, for its roots are too deep. With AIDS becoming rampant, the world is at last realizing that sin is suicide. But fear of hell is powerless to save from it.

Hope of reward is equally ineffective, hence the large percentage of "religion-conscious" girls and boys who yield to temptation. Abounding sin needs *much more* abounding grace—a revelation of the closeness of the Savior, an awareness that passes through the mind and penetrates to the inner heart. Only those who have received the atonement can be successful in ministering that grace to youth. But the glorious message of Christ's righteousness comes into its own to meet the need.

It was God Himself who created us male and female and endowed us with sexual attraction. And He then pronounced this "very good." Sex preceded sin; therefore sin cannot be inherent in sex within marriage. There is sin only in its selfish, godless perversion.

But through many centuries of wandering from the truth of the gospel, the great enemy has invested sex with an aura of shame and inherent sin. Thus as we saw in the words of Fulton Sheen comes the idea of an "Immaculate Conception" for the Virgin Mary. It makes her so "unique," he says, that "in Mary, there was hardly any earth at all." This is a polite way of saying that she was not a normal sexual human being. In her nature "all was Heaven," he adds. As her Son, Sheen's "Christ" must also be "desolidarized and separated," "exempt," from our sexual humanity. He must know nothing of our God-given sexuality. This perversion of truth derives from the pagan, Hellenistic, and evolutionary concept of sex as purely an animal instinct.

In contrast the Bible presents a divine Savior who took on Himself our full corporate humanity, "yet without sin." To believe in Him includes thanking Him for creating us male and female, praising Him for the gift of sex within marriage, rejoicing in our sexuality. Through faith we yield it to Him that He may sanctify it and make it a lifelong source of joy, free from the poison of guilt or shame, permitting the pure love of *agape* to motivate it.

Such faith refocuses the Ten Commandments. "Thou shalt not commit adultery" becomes no longer a kill-joy prohibition but a promise of victory over illicit, selfish sex. It is transformed into an assurance that Christ's unselfish love (which "does no harm to a neighbor," Romans 13:10) can always control us. Result? Genuine happiness.

The Practical Value of Christ's Nearness to Us

Many are asking, How can I get close to Jesus? The first step is to believe how close He has come to you. Then the next step follows naturally: the honest heart that appreciates that closeness *identifies with Him on His cross*. Paul said (according to the original language) that his *ego* is "crucified with Christ" (Galatians 2:20).

Of course, this does not mean that the one who believes in Christ grovels ever after in the dust of self-depreciation. His sense of self-respect is never shattered. To be "crucified with Christ" means also to be resurrected with Him; "it is no longer I who live, but Christ lives in me." Now one finds his truest self-respect. David says, "He pulled me out of a dangerous pit, out of the deadly quicksand. He set me safely on a rock and made me secure" (Psalm 40:2, GNB).

And with pouring contempt on all our pride comes the utter repudiation of all "holier-than-thou" feelings. The closer one comes to Christ, the more sinful and unworthy he feels himself to be. We are never to judge ourselves, or give ourselves grade-points. We are never to claim to be sinless, for "if we say that we have no sin, we deceive ourselves, and the truth is not in us." It is only when we continually "confess our sins, [that] He is faithful and just to forgive us our sins, and to cleanse us from all unrighteousness" (1 John 1:8, 9).

The proud and arrogant heresy of perfectionism can never rear its ugly head where the truth of Christ's righteousness is appreciated, for the song of every heart will be to glory alone in "CHRIST OUR RIGHTEOUSNESS."

CHAPTER ELEVEN

The Glorious Good News of the New Covenant

The Good News of the new covenant is an essential part of the gospel message. The apostle Paul says that the confusion of the old covenant ideas "gives birth to bondage" (Galatians 4:24). For many years these old covenant ideas have held the ascendancy while we have mostly been unaware of what they are. That widespread "bondage" is one reason why so many youth rebel against what they think is the gospel.

In 1738 John Wesley chanced on a meeting where someone was reading what Luther wrote about righteousness by faith. Wesley said, "I did feel my heart strangely warmed." Many who have gained an understanding of the two covenants have testified that it brings a brilliant insight into a happier life. In this chapter we wish to let the Bible unfold this precious message. May your heart also be "strangely warmed" by this beautiful truth.

The New Covenant Is God's Promise

Long before the "old covenant" came into being, the Lord originally made the promise that constitutes the new covenant. This "everlasting covenant" was made before the foundation of the world, containing the same promise as the new covenant. It is God's promise to make His people "complete in every good work to do His will ... through Jesus Christ" (Hebrews 13:20, 21; Genesis 17:7; Revelation 13:8). That is a big project, because not only have all mankind sinned, but they have fallen into a slavery to sin and *ego*-centeredness so deep that the roots penetrate to the depths of our psyche. The new covenant is the news of how God solves this problem and provides full healing.

Theologians talk about the Adamic covenant, the Noachian covenant, and the Abrahamic covenant, but these are all the same "new" or "everlasting covenant" that God promised, only under different circumstances. There is no need to be confused by artificial definitions. The principle and the promise are always the same—what the Lord does for us.

This covenant (or promise) was made more distinct and far-reaching in His conversations with Abraham. He virtually promised the old man the sky! The Lord would give his descendants land "northward, southward, eastward, and westward." "Count the stars if you are able to number them; so shall your descendants be." In him "all the families of the earth shall be blessed" (Genesis 12:1-3; 13:14-17; 15:5, 6).

These staggering promises amount to total blessing:

(1) Abraham's descendants will become the greatest nation in the world.

(2) The Messiah will come through them.

(3) They will bring happiness and prosperity to every family in the world.

(4) The land of Canaan will be their possession.

(5) More than that, the promise includes the whole world, which must mean the New Earth after God re-creates it (cf. Romans 4:13).

(6) Since the earth is to be an "everlasting possession," the covenant must include everlasting life as well (John 3:16).

(7) Moreover, since only righteousness can dwell in this new earth (2 Peter 3:13), the new covenant promise includes making righteous all who believe.

(8) The down payment on all this incredible blessing would be a miraculous birth (Genesis 17:1-8, 21; 18:14; Romans 4:11), enabling Abraham's aged and sterile wife Sarah to have a son whose name is to be Isaac ("laughter").

(9) The world's Savior is not to come through Ishmael, who is a symbol of an old covenant do-it-yourself works-program, but

(10) Christ will come through Isaac's descent, and this will forever demonstrate that Abraham's true descendants are only those who have his faith.

What promises did God ask Abraham to make in return? If you read carefully, you will see that the answer is—none! The new covenant promise is entirely one-sided. God does all the promising. He does not ask us to make promises to Him, for He knows we cannot keep them.

But was Abraham expected to *do nothing*? What was his part in the bargain? The answer is an astounding one that many people have trouble with: only one thing, *believe*. "He believed in the Lord, and He accounted it to him for righteousness" (Genesis 15:5, 6). To be honest, we must recognize that all the Lord has ever asked from anyone is what He asked from Abraham: *faith*.

This does not mean that He did not *expect* obedience, or that good works were not important. The Lord was teaching Abraham the principle of righteousness by faith. Once Abraham learned to *believe*, true obedience would follow as surely as fruit follows the blossom. And it did, for the Lord said later, "I have known him ... to do righteousness and justice" (Genesis 18:19)

The ancient Jews misunderstood the new covenant, because circumcision became for them the symbol of their do-it-yourself, works-and-obedience program. But the Apostle Paul got to the heart of it. His point is neat: Abraham's faith was "accounted ... to him for righteousness" (Romans 4:3).

Brilliant insight! This is how the apostle proved that justification is by faith alone. Six times in Romans 4 we read that Abraham is "*our father*," the spiritual ancestor of all who exercise faith, Jews or Gentiles.

But Paul is not putting down obedience, for the word "righteousness" means true justification. The word implies straightening out what was crooked, being put right, that is, learning genuine obedience. Such obedience becomes possible only by faith, but the Good News is that it is not only possible, *but certain if like Abraham we will believe God's magnificent promise.*

God's Covenant Is the Same as His One–sided Promise

The truth of the two covenants discloses a beautiful garden where others see only a barren desert:

> The covenant and promise of God are one and the same. ...
> God's covenants with men can be nothing else than promises
> to them. ...

After the Flood God made a covenant with every beast of the earth, and with every fowl; but the beasts and the birds did not promise anything in return. Genesis 9:9-16. They simply received the favor at the hand of God. That is all we can do—receive. God promises us everything that we need, and more than we can ask or think, as a gift. We give Him ourselves, that is, nothing. And He gives us Himself, that is, everything. That which makes all the trouble is that even when men are willing to recognize the Lord at all they want to make bargains with Him. They want it to be an equal, "mutual" affair—a transaction in which they can consider themselves on a par with God. ...

The gospel was as full and complete in the days of Abraham as it has ever been or ever will be. No addition to it or change in its provisions or conditions could possibly be made after God's oath to Abraham. Nothing can be taken away from it as it thus existed, and not one thing can ever be required from any man more than what was required of Abraham.[1]

Could anything be more difficult than making dead people come alive? But that is what the One specializes in who promises us the new covenant. He "gives life to the dead and calls those things which do not exist as though they did" (Romans 4:13, 14, 16-18). In other words, He already counts for you as reality blessings that you have not yet even begun to see. When we learn to believe His Good News, we too will "call those things which do not exist as though they did," because the Word of God declares that these apparently impossible blessings will be. Can you begin to see how the new covenant is the perfect antidote for depression?

How the Old Covenant Came In

When the Lord brought Israel out of Egyptian slavery, He wanted to impress on their minds the same covenant He had made long before with their father Abraham:

You have seen what I did to the Egyptians, and how I bore you on eagles' wings and brought you to Myself. Now therefore, if you will indeed obey My voice and keep My covenant, then you shall be a special treasure to Me above

---

1. E. J. Waggoner, *The Glad Tidings*, pp. 71, 73; CFI ed. (2016).

all people for all the earth is Mine. And you shall be to Me a kingdom of priests and a holy nation (Exodus 19:3, 4).

The Hebrew word for "obey" means "listen." Any parent knows that obedience is easier for the child if he will listen. Since God's covenant is always His promise, to "keep My covenant" means to cherish and to appreciate the promise He made to their forefather, Abraham. The Hebrew word here translated "keep" is *shamar*, used of Adam who was to "tend and keep" the Garden of Eden (Genesis 2:15). Adam *cherished* or *appreciated* the Garden. The Lord was asking Israel at Sinai to cherish or appreciate the promise He made to their father Abraham.

In other words, if Israel at Sinai would *believe* the Lord as Abraham did, they would become a "kingdom of priests, and a holy nation," the greatest on earth. They would never know failure or defeat. The whole world would beat a path to their door to learn about righteousness by faith which solves all human problems. "If they would simply keep God's covenant, keep the faith, and believe God's promise, they would be a 'peculiar treasure' unto God."[2]

To "bear ... on eagle's wings" is the meaning of the Latin word from which we get our word "succor." We read in the King James Version that Christ "is able to succour them that are tempted" (Hebrews 2:18). The deliverance from Egypt was designed to teach this same new covenant truth—that the Lord saves us like a mother eagle saves her young. Israel did nothing to effect their deliverance from Egypt except to *let* the Lord do it for them, as a baby eagle lets its mother succor it. But the people did not understand the lesson. They wanted a works-program.

Obsessed with legalism, they permitted unbelief to blind their souls so that they could not appreciate God's grace as Abraham did. Their response was not like his, to *believe* with a contrite heart. Instead, they solemnly promised to be good, that they would obey: "Then all the people answered together and said, 'All that the Lord has spoken we will do'" (Exodus 19:8). *This was the old covenant.* It was the promise of the people:

> These two covenants exist today. The two covenants are not matters of time, but of condition. Let no one flatter himself that he cannot be bound under the old covenant,

2. Ibid., p. 99.

thinking that its time has passed. The time for that is passed only in the sense that "the time past of our life may suffice us to have wrought the will of the Gentiles, when we walked in lasciviousness, lusts, excess of wine, revelings, banquetings, and abominable idolatries" (1 Peter 4:3, KJV).[3]

This promise of "all the people" necessitated a detour occasioned by their unbelief. If the people would not keep step with Him, the Lord must now humble Himself to keep step with them. He must ratify their old covenant in order to show them the futility of their self-confidence and legalism.

Paul says that the "law ... was added because of transgressions" (Galatians 3:19). The word "added" means "emphasized," "underlined," or "articulated":

> The law was given to show them [Israel] that they had not faith and so were not true children of Abraham, and were therefore in a fair way to lose the inheritance. God would have put His law into their hearts even as He put it into Abraham's heart, if they had believed. But when they disbelieved, yet still professed to be heirs of the promise, it was necessary to show them in the most marked manner that their unbelief was sin. ... They had the same spirit as their descendants, who asked, "What must we *do*, to be doing the work of God?" John 6:28, RSV. ... Unless they saw their sin, they could not avail themselves of the promise. Hence the necessity of the speaking of the law.[4]

Now must come the terrors of Mount Sinai, which were completely unnecessary for Abraham. Since the people had now instituted the old covenant by making their arrogant promise, the Lord was obliged to communicate His law to them through a different method (Exodus 19:16-18; 20:1-20). He did not need to frighten Abraham with thunders and lightnings and earthquakes, for He wrote His holy law in his believing heart. The old covenant depends on fear as its motivation to produce "the works of the law," because the motivation of faith has not yet been realized.

For example, to refrain from illicit sex because of fear of AIDS or because of shame is old covenant legalism. To keep the Sabbath

---

3. Ibid., p. 100.
4. Ibid., p. 74.

because of fear of being lost is also legalism. It is good to refrain from illicit sex, and it is good to keep the Sabbath, but the motive that is truly effective is supplied only by the grace of God in the new covenant.

The new covenant is heart-religion, an inexpressible gratitude and awe imposed by grace. The Lord promises, "I will put My laws in their mind and write them on their hearts" (cf. Hebrews 8:8-12). This means more than memorizing Bible verses. It means a love-affair with truth.

How does the Lord write His law in human hearts? It's easy to answer glibly, "By the Holy Spirit." But how does He do it? By capturing the affections of the soul, what people long ago often said is "heart-work." The alienated heart is reconciled to God through that "blood of the cross." When "the love of Christ constrains us" we become new creatures (2 Corinthians 5:14-21). The cold stony heart we were born with becomes melted; a new spirit fills the heart. We learn to hate the sins we once loved, and we love harmony and reconciliation with the Savior.

Under the new covenant, the Ten Commandments become ten glorious promises. For example, says the Lord, when you *believe* that "I am the Lord your God, who brought you out of the land of Egypt, out of the house of bondage," inexpressible gratitude will motivate you. Then you shall never fall into adultery, or into murder, or into stealing, or any other sin. An appreciation of that cross cleanses those buried motivations of sin and selfishness that have such deep roots. This is how the new covenant bears fruit.

The fruit cannot be the cold "works of the law" that are motivated by fear; it is a selfless devotion to Christ which alone is true obedience. "*Agape* is the fulfilling of the law" (Romans 13:10).

> God's precepts are promises; they *must* necessarily be such, because He knows that we have no power. All that God requires is what He gives. When He says, "Thou shalt not" we may take it as His assurance that if we but believe Him He will preserve us from the sin against which He warns us.[5]

The Common but Terrible Bondage of the Old Covenant

Making old covenant promises to God "gives birth to bondage," says Paul. If s a terrible thing to drag unsuspecting young Christians

---

5. Ibid., p. 77.

into this spiritual bondage. But this is what happens when we lead them to make these vain promises to God.

For example, children and youth are led to promise to keep the Ten Commandments "every day," and never to go where those commandments tell them "no." Soon they forget or someone entices them into a mistake. They realize that they have broken their promise, and their failures alienate them from the grace of God. Having broken their promise, they feel that they are no good. They feel that they cannot trust their own sincerity and they conclude that they have not been "elected" to be saved. The problem is that God never asked them to make a promise in the first place. Some few may find their way back from the bondage of the old covenant into the liberty of the new, but many others fall and never rise again.

It is not only useless but harmful to lead children to promise God that they will keep the Ten Commandments, that they will never go where they shouldn't, or that they will be obedient forever. *Not that it is wrong to obey.* The problem is that the old covenant is not *the way* to obey. For example, it is well known that it is useless to lead a cigarette addict to promise never to smoke again, or an alcoholic to promise never to drink again. The true secret is making a right choice, which is possible only through grace.

There are still lethal injections of old covenant ideas that lace Christian literature for children and youth, and the bondage thus ministered is one reason why so many become discouraged. A deeply perceptive author tells us the root reason why the old covenant leads into spiritual bondage:

> You are weak in moral power, in slavery to doubt, and controlled by the habits of your life of sin. Your promises and resolutions are like ropes of sand. You cannot control your thoughts, your impulses, your affections. The knowledge of your broken promises and forfeited pledges weakens your confidence in your own sincerity, and causes you to feel that God cannot accept you [this is what Paul means when he says that the old covenant "gives birth to bondage"]; ... What you need to understand is the true force of the will. ... Everything depends on the right action of the will. ... You cannot change your heart, you cannot of yourself give to God its affections; but you can *choose* to serve Him. ... Thus your whole nature will be brought under the control of the

Spirit of Christ; your affections will be centered upon Him, your thoughts will be in harmony with Him.[6]

Even some of our beloved hymns are permeated with old covenant concepts that "give birth to bondage." The effect is often subliminal. Sincere Christians are unconsciously enslaved by darkness and depression assimilated from respected hymns or "gospel" songs that convey "under the law" or *ego*-oriented messages.

The Mighty Power of the Holy Spirit

Our Savior administers His new covenant promise through the ministry of the Holy Spirit. The pope of Rome claims to be the Vicar of Christ, His representative on earth, taking His place since Christ has ascended to heaven. If that were true, it would be bad news for everyone, for the pope can do nothing to help you and me so far as salvation from sin is concerned. He is too far away and too busy with too many problems.

Jesus said that His true Vicar on earth is the Holy Spirit. That is Good News, because He can help you and me even more than Jesus could if He were here in person. In fact, He is called the Spirit of Christ, Christ's Representative, divested of physical limitations but acting in His stead.

The three Persons of the Godhead are one God. That is why Jesus said that when the Holy Spirit comes, *He* comes, not personally as when He returns in the clouds of heaven, but in the Spirit.

As our previous chapter reveals, Jesus is closer to us than popular teaching allows; so the Holy Spirit is also closer to us than we have thought. He is as much a Friend as Jesus is. He is on our side, trying to get us ready to enter heaven, not trying to keep us out.

Jesus introduces the Holy Spirit by giving Him a special name—"another Helper" (John 14:16-18, 26). He is "another *parakletos*," that is, a Replacement for Himself. He is sent "in My name." The Greek word means "the one who is called to come and sit down beside you forever" (*para*, as in parallel—two railroad tracks are parallel, and they always stay together; and *kletos*, the One called). He will never leave us, although we have power to grieve Him and drive Him off if we choose. We are closer to Christ today by the Spirit than the Twelve were 2000 years ago when they walked and talked with Him personally.

---

6. Ellen G. White, *Steps to Christ*, Pacific Press Publishing Association, p. 47.

The Holy Spirit is also a Master Teacher and Stimulator of our memory, for Jesus said that "He will teach you all things, and bring to your remembrance all things that I said to you" (John 14:26).

Why did Jesus have to go away personally? "It is to your advantage that I go away; for if I do not go away, the Helper will not come to you; but if I depart, I will send Him to you" (John 16:7-11). If He had remained here personally or physically, He would have been our Pope (I speak reverently), but limited by physical existence. You or I could not have a visit with Him except by going through His secretaries and waiting for months or years for a few precious minutes with Him. Many of earth's billions could never visit with Him at all.

But through the Holy Spirit each of us has unlimited access to Christ as though we were each the only human being on earth. The Holy Spirit is God the Spirit, Christ the Spirit, everywhere at once. He has nearly eight billion people to care for, but He is *infinite*. Thus He gives full attention to each one of us. He notices when even a sparrow falls. Like standing in the bright sunshine; you couldn't get more of Him if you were the only person in the world.

The Good News of the Holy Spirit's work in the new covenant shines brightly. When we understand how good the Good News is, we discover that it is easy to be saved and it is hard to be lost. Under the reign of grace it is as easy to do right as under the reign of sin it is easy to do wrong. This must be so; for if there is not more power in grace than there is in sin, then there can be no salvation from sin.

Let no one ever attempt to serve God with anything less than the present, living power of God that makes him a new creature. Then the service of God will indeed be in "newness of life"; then it will be seen that His yoke is "easy" and his burden "light." His service will be with "joy inexpressible and full of glory" (see Matthew 11:28-30; Romans 5:20, 21; 6:4; 2 Corinthians 5:17; 1 Peter 1:8).

Boundless grace is given to every one, bringing salvation in full measure. If any one does not have that blessing, why is it? Plainly it can be only because he will not take that which is given. Unbelief is the problem.

When we read or hear the word of God, we are to open the heart to that word, that it may accomplish the will of God in us. The word of God itself is to do the work, and we are to let it. "*Let* the word of Christ dwell in you richly in all wisdom," says the apostle (Colossians 3:16).

Perhaps we never realized it before, but the Good News declares that it is actually hard work to be lost. Christ specifically says that His "yoke is easy" and to resist His grace is "hard" (Matthew 11:28-30; Acts 26:14).

Good News to the Last Page

The last page of the Bible extends the final invitation, "The Spirit and the bride say, Come" (Revelation 22:17). The Spirit is appealing to people who we may think are hopeless, and the church which is to be the Bride of Christ is to be in perfect sympathy with Him in His concern for them. Many more than we suppose will respond. God's true, honest people are still in the darkness of the world. They will take the place of those who will leave Christ in the last great crisis, who have long professed the gospel but have rejected it in heart because they have resisted the kind of self-crucified devotion to Christ that the cross demands.

Angels and the Holy Spirit still cooperate in holding back the final outburst of strife and plagues symbolized by the loosing of the "four winds" (Revelation 7:1-4). You cannot safely drive down the highway unless the Holy Spirit restrains some drunk or drug-crazed maniac from plowing into you. The entire world would be engulfed in ruin unless the Holy Spirit were restraining the evil that is about to burst loose.

But He is being withdrawn from the world, not because He wants to leave but because mankind is steadily driving Him off. "Today if you will hear His voice, do not harden your hearts" (Hebrews 3:7, 8). The final sin against Him which is unpardonable is that last choice to reject His pleading when He says, "This is the way, walk in it." If we reject His conviction of sin and the remembrance of truth, then He is grieved and is forced to turn away forever. We are all rapidly coming to a final choice—to go all the way with the Holy Spirit and be sealed for the coming of the Lord, or to make a last choice to reject Him.

Only one thing is truly difficult for us—and that is to believe how good the Good News is. Our constant battle is to "fight the good fight of faith" (1 Timothy 6:12). Mankind is so held captive to unbelief that nothing can break through those chains except the truth of the cross of Christ and the full reality of the Holy Spirit's constant ministry. He is still the Vicar of the great High Priest who is cleansing the Heavenly Sanctuary.

His Good News is powerful. Stop resisting Him. *Let* Him lead you all the way home.

"Natural" Immortality— A Key Deception

Did Christ Really Die on His Cross? *Agape* versus the Doctrine of "Natural" Immortality

Alexander D. Snyman

Once there is a departure from truth in any area of Scriptural teaching there follows a seemingly endless train of repercussions as one by one other doctrines of the Bible are affected. This is inevitable, since Biblical Truth is an entity which cannot be divided and put into pockets. The various doctrines of the Bible overlap and interlock over and over, each one is related to all the others. In fact, it is particularly true of the popular teaching of the "natural immortality" of the soul,[1] because once this teaching is embraced, the mind is immediately closed to a clear understanding of many other truths of the Scriptures. It is our purpose in this presentation to consider some of those tenets most central to the Gospel message which are affected by the immortal-soul idea.

First to be considered will be the teaching of the Scriptures concerning the resurrection. Preaching on this subject has virtually disappeared from the popular pulpits, and with good reason! If, as is generally taught, the righteous go to heaven at death, then why the

---

1. "Natural" immortality is generally understood to refer to the survival of the "soul," or "spiritual part" of the human being, that is assumed to persist after death of the individual in some other state apart from the physical body.

need of a resurrection later? Any attempts to resolve the difficulty by telling of a later reunion of the "soul" with a resurrected body brings only added confusion. It is easier to leave the matter of the resurrection alone.

However, to ignore the resurrection doctrine is to bypass one of the most central points of emphasis in the New Testament. When our Lord returns to this earth, the apostle Paul tells us, He will "descend from heaven with a shout, with the voice of the archangel, and with the trump of God: and the dead in Christ shall rise first" (1 Thessalonians 4:16).* This is the voice of Christ Himself. Once, speaking to the Jews, Jesus said, "Marvel not at this: for the hour is coming, in the which all that are in the graves shall hear His voice, and shall come forth; they that have done good, unto the resurrection of life; and they that have done evil, unto the resurrection of damnation" (John 5:28, 29).

Those who are resurrected come forth from death, not from life in some celestial paradise. They come up from the graves, not down from heaven. They emerge from a state of unconsciousness, not from an environment of bliss inhabited by vaporous beings. Were they to be recalled from any state of consciousness this could hardly be called a resurrection from the dead. Death implies absence of life, and thus of consciousness.

Paul the apostle lays great stress upon the doctrine of the resurrection. In his defense before Felix, the governor, he said, "there *shall be a resurrection of the dead, both of the just and the unjust*" (Acts 24:15). And addressing King Agrippa he asked, "Why should it be thought a thing incredible with you, that God should raise the dead?" (Acts 26:8). But his profoundest treatment of the subject of the resurrection is given in his letter to the Corinthians, chapter fifteen. Virtually the entire chapter is devoted to driving home this wonderful truth, that the righteous dead are to be raised, and upon them will be conferred "incorruptibility" and "immortality" (verses 51-54). Paul's reasoning in this chapter is conclusive. If there is no resurrection of the dead, he argues, then "*Christ is not risen,*" and if this is the case then "*our preaching is vain,*" "*we are false witnesses,*" and "*your faith is vain*" (verses 12-17). Also, "*they which are fallen asleep in Christ are perished,*" and "*we are of all men most miserable*" (verses 18, 19). He points out further that there would be no point in a Christian's exposing

---

* The King James Version is used throughout this Appendix.

himself to danger or death were there no resurrection to which to look forward. We may as well *eat and drink, for tomorrow we die* (verses 30-32). In other words, get all you can out of this life, for it is all you will have. Thus the apostle Paul proves how vital to sound Christian doctrine the fact of the resurrection from the dead really is.

All of these arguments not only destroy the idea that there is no resurrection of the dead, but also makes completely incompatible with the resurrection doctrine the idea of a separate conscious existence of "soul" or "spirit." It is one or the other. The doctrine of the resurrection and the doctrine of the immortality of the soul are mutually exclusive.

Parallel to this question of the resurrection is the whole matter of the disposition of evil and the punishment of evildoers. Belief in the natural immortality of the soul requires a corresponding belief in the perpetuation of sin and sinners throughout the ceaseless ages of eternity, and this in turn requires a belief in a punishment which begins at death and goes on forever. According to this idea, once sin has entered the world, it can never be eliminated. If sinners already possess immortality then God Himself is unable to blot them out of existence. So forever and ever, while ransomed souls sing the praises of Him who created and redeemed, lost souls are giving vent to their feelings of agony and frustration with screams and curses which will be heard throughout eternity. There will never come a time when good and evil, joy and pain, love and hate, life and death will not continue side by side in God's kingdom.

Happily, the Scriptures do not paint such a picture of things to come. We are told of a judgment yet future. Solomon ends his witness to the world with these words: "Fear God and keep His commandments: for this is the whole duty of man. For God shall bring every work into judgment, with every secret thing, whether it be good, or whether it be evil" (Ecclesiastes 12:13, 14). This statement alone is enough to prove that lost sinners are not being punished now. There exists no place of torment now, nor will there be until the end of the world, and then only long enough to exterminate all sin and its effects. The dead are now in their graves, perfectly unconscious. This doctrine of the natural immortality of the soul carries with it the necessary corollary that punishment is going on now in a fiery inferno. But if the judgment is yet future, then it can only be concluded that there are untold millions suffering, some already for millenniums of time, who may learn one day that a mistake has been made in their cases, and they should have been in heaven instead of hell! Or we could ask, "Why a future judgment if judgment has already been rendered"?

Solomon is not the only one of the Bible writers who tell of a future judgment. We read, "It is appointed unto men once to die, but after this the judgment." (Hebrews 9:27). And Job says, "For ye say, Where is the house of the prince? And where are the dwelling places of the wicked? Have ye not asked them that go by the way? And do ye not know their tokens, that the wicked is reserved to the day of destruction? They shall be brought forth to the day of wrath" (Job 21:28-30). Essentially the same thought is echoed by Peter: "For if God spared not the angels that sinned, but cast them down to hell, and delivered them into chains of darkness, to be reserved unto judgment. … The Lord knoweth how to deliver the godly out of temptations, and to reserve the unjust unto the day of judgment to be punished" (2 Peter 2:4, 9). And Jude tells us: "And Enoch also, the seventh from Adam, prophesied of these, saying, Behold, the Lord cometh with ten thousands of His saints, to execute judgment upon all, and to convince all that are ungodly among them of all their ungodly deeds which they have ungodly committed" (Jude 14, 15). Isaiah places the judgment in the future: "And it shall come to pass in that day, that the Lord shall punish the host of the high ones that are on high, and the kings of the earth upon the earth" (Isaiah 24:21). Our Lord Himself taught a judgment yet to come: "For the Son of man shall come in the glory of His Father with His angels; and then He shall reward every man according to his works" (Matthew 16:27). And again: "He that rejecteth me, and receiveth not my words, hath One that judgeth him: the word that I have spoken, the same shall judge him in the last day" (John 12:48).

A belief in the soul's natural immortality is at variance with all these texts, and many more which could be cited. For reasons already given, it is impossible to reconcile the idea of men who have died continuing in a state of consciousness somewhere, whether of bliss or torment, implying that in their cases judgment has already been rendered, with the clear teaching of the Scriptures that the judgment is still in the future. Like the tentacles of some cancer, this key deception, the doctrine of natural immortality, reaches everywhere, and destroys the entire structure of Bible truth regarding God's plan for this world.

Serious as are these invasions into the various areas of truth, probably in none does the immortal soul teaching affect our understanding of the Gospel so much as it does in the area of the Atonement. Clearly, "the wages of sin is death" (Romans 6:23). And again, "The soul that sinneth, it shall die" (Ezekiel 18:20). "Sin, when it is finished, bringeth forth death" (James 1:15).

We do not read that the wages of sin is eternal torment in the fires of hell, but death, which is the complete absence of life and consciousness, the final and complete extinction of being. "Wherefore, as by one man sin entered into the world, and death by sin; and so death passed upon all men, for that all have sinned" (Romans 5:12). Thus all are under the death penalty because of sin. "But God commendeth His love toward us, in that, while we were yet sinners, Christ died for us" (Romans 5:8). Redemption, atonement, can be accomplished only by having Someone die in the place of fallen man, and thus effect the reconciliation which means salvation for all who choose to respond to this demonstration of God's love. "For if, when we were enemies, we were reconciled to God by the death of His Son, much more, being reconciled, we shall be saved by His life. And not only so, but we also joy in God through our Lord Jesus Christ, by whom we have now received the atonement" (Romans 5:10, 11). Upon the Substitute, the Surety, were our sins placed, for "the Lord hath laid on Him the iniquity of us all" (Isaiah 53:6).

Central to the salvation theme is the fact that Christ took upon Himself the penalty for sin which we would have had to suffer. It is the one golden thread which runs all the way through the sacred pages of the Scriptures. As Ellen G. White tells it:

> Christ was treated as we deserve, that we might be treated as He deserves. He was condemned for our sins, in which He had no share, that we might be justified by His righteousness, in which we had no share. He suffered the death which was ours, that we might receive the life which was His. "With His stripes we are healed."[2]

Now if the "wages of sin is death," and Christ made full atonement for us on the cross, it is obvious that His agony and death on Calvary fully satisfied the demands of Heaven's justice in meeting the problem of a transgressed law. But if, as some claim, sinners are to be tortured

2. Ellen G. White, *The Desire of Ages*, p. 25.

in a flaming cauldron for all eternity because of their sins, the question immediately arises, Why is Christ not now suffering the agony of eternal torment, if such is indeed the penalty for sin? For to save this lost world God saw that it was necessary for a Substitute to be provided who would take upon Himself the total guilt and punishment for the sin of the entire human race, and that only in this way could mankind be saved. Thus the fact that Christ is not now suffering eternal torment should be enough to show that "the wages of sin is death" and not everlasting agony in the fires of hell.

However, someone may ask here, and reasonably, If Christ did not take upon Himself eternal torment, is it not equally true that He did not suffer the penalty of eternal death, but is even now alive, and at the right hand of the Father? Certainly when the Bible tells us that *"the wages of sin is death,"* this has to mean eternal death, eternal separation from God, not death for a time and then a joyous resurrection. Otherwise the wicked, raised to life at the close of the thousand years (Revelation 20:5, 7, 8) could rightly say, *"We have already died once. We have paid the price for our sins. It is not right that we should die again."* The answer, very simply, is that death as the wages of sin means forever and ever, for all eternity. But then how can it be said that Christ died for our sins, and paid the full price for our sins, thus effecting a full and complete atonement, and yet was resurrected the third day and has been alive ever since?

This question brings us not only to the heart of Atonement, but to the very heart of God, the revelation of His character, the virtual center point of the universe. It involves an understanding of the great love motif of the Word of God, an area which has been, sad to say, very much neglected and also greatly misunderstood. This will be considered in a little more detail.

Different words for "love" appeared in Greek over the early centuries. In Platonic times *eros* was the highest concept of Greek philosophical thought, a love of the purest, noblest, kind. But *eros* was based upon a self centered concept, and so could not rise above the level of man's highest capabilities, which, being sin based, could not ascend to the point of a true grasp of the love which the New Testament writers were attempting to portray. In fact, the direction of *eros* could only be downward, so that by New Testament times its meaning had degraded to a level of baseness. It was completely unsuitable for New Testament use.

Other words for "love" made their appearances: *storgos*, a word with a very narrow meaning, which is found only twice in the New Testament in its combinative form *astorgos* (without natural affection, Romans 1:31, 2 Timothy 3:3), and *philos*, which appears many times in its various forms (verb *phileo*), and which indicates a warm, tender love of a friend or close family member. This word finds a place in the New Testament where the closeness and tenderness of members of the Christian family is described.

But what developed into the great love word of the New Testament was the word *agape* (ah-GAH-pay). Comparatively obscure at the time, it nevertheless came to embody a meaning which made it unique even among all the love words of the world's languages. Other languages today, English included, have to explain its meaning since there is no equivalent word in any language anywhere on earth. *Agape* means essentially *ultimate selflessness. It makes all consideration for personal well-being entirely secondary.* This means that, if necessary, such love would choose complete self-emptying, eternal loss, eternal negation, eternal death. *Agape* described the very character of God. "*God is agape (love)*" (John 4:8).

Could this explain what really happened on the cross of Calvary? Remember, for Christ to redeem a lost world required that He pay the price for sin completely. He must stand before God in the sinner's place, and thus be put in the position of a condemned sinner and no longer a beloved Son. He would then have to bear God's frown for disobedience and wrath against sin and no longer His love for His only Son. This in turn meant that He must die, be deprived of life and consciousness, not just for three days and three nights, but forever. Further, this meant that all hope of a glad resurrection and reunion with His Father in heaven must be abandoned. Any thought of ever again enjoying the environment of heaven must be set aside completely. To take the sinner's place meant that He must endure the agony of eternal separation from God. The penalty for the transgression of a holy and just law involved all this and much more.

Agape is a love so great that the Godhead was willing to have all this take place on the cross of Calvary in order to make redemption for lost souls possible. And remember that the Father did not suffer any less than did the Son in that agony of Gethsemane and Calvary.

Now, did all this, and more, actually take place in the Atonement?

Can it be averred that Christ on the cross of Calvary did indeed pay a price for man's redemption, which was in every way equivalent to the eternal death which the penalty for sin required? Fortunately, to this question we can reply, "Yes, in every way!"

Consider how Ellen G. White described the agony of our Lord on the cross:

> Satan with his fierce temptations wrung the heart of Jesus. The Saviour could not see through the portals of the tomb. Hope did not present to Him His coming forth from the grave a conqueror, or tell Him of the Father's acceptance of the sacrifice. He feared that sin was so offensive to God that their separation was to be eternal. Christ felt the anguish which the sinner will feel when mercy shall no longer plead for the guilty race.[3]

Simply put, we can say that Christ died the equivalent of the second death on the cross of Calvary, the death from which there is no resurrection (see Revelation 20:6, 9, 14) Further we are told:

> The withdrawal of the divine countenance from the Saviour in this hour of supreme anguish pierced His heart with a sorrow that can never be fully understood by man. So great was this agony that His physical pain was hardly felt.[4]

Many there are in the Christian world today who do not begin to understand what happened on Calvary. To them the Atonement involved no more than the physical agonies of a crucifixion. Terrible as these are, they do not, by any stretch of the imagination, stand in the same category as those mental and emotional agonies which Christ endured. Many believe that Jesus and the penitent thief enjoyed a glad reunion in the realms of glory only minutes after the crucifixion itself. And what is at the bottom of this serious error is the doctrine of natural immortality. This is why, in the matter of the Atonement more than any other, this doctrine is seen to be the key deception that it is. Or to put it another way, *it can be said that there is no way in which the Atonement can be fully understood by any who believe in the doctrine of the soul's natural immortality.*

---

3. *The Desire of Ages*, p. 753.
4. Ibid., p. 753.

Agape, and its antithesis, *eros*, have been critically researched by Anders Nygren, a Swedish Lutheran bishop, in his book *Agape and Eros*. It is a classic in its field. And it is interesting to note that Nygren finds no possible room for an immortal soul doctrine, or any of its related tenets or philosophies, in the *agape* motif of the New Testament. He says in one significant paragraph:

> This conception of the double nature of man, of the Divine origin and quality of the soul, its liberation from the things of sense, and its ascent to its original Divine home, is the common basis on which every theory of Eros rests. Around this basic idea, however, a whole series of characteristic ideas group themselves, all intimately connected with the Eros motif, such as belief in a pre-existent Fall, the conception of the body as the prison house of the soul, the idea of the transmigration of souls, belief in the soul's natural immortality; and hand in hand with these go the basic mood of asceticism and the mystical-ecstatic way of salvation.[5]

Anders Nygren's study of *agape*, the love-motif of the New Testament, leads him to reject completely all these pagan philosophies, including the teaching of the soul's natural immortality, as being irreconcilable with the character of God's love as revealed on the cross. Instead he finds that these heathen ideas are all *eros*-based, and *eros*, as we have noted, finds no place in the New Testament. Obviously, any who have come to understand Christ's atonement on the cross fully, will find it impossible to accept the doctrine of natural immortality.

A beautiful, heaven-sent antidote for the terrible deceptions which have held captive so many minds in the Christian communion is the 1888 message of Christ's righteousness. With its emphasis upon the vital themes of salvation, the message of A.T. Jones and E.J. Waggoner presents the New Testament Gospel in a light not seen since apostolic times.[6] And while neither Ellen G. White nor Jones nor Waggoner ever used the word *agape*, their whole message is vibrant with the *agape* theme. To give this message to the peoples of earth, "*the message*

---

5. Anders Nygren, *Agape and Eros,* The Westminster Press, Philadelphia (1953), p. 164.
6. Ellen G. White, *Fundamentals of Christian Education*, p. 473.

that God commanded to be given to the world,"[7] is to present the truths of the Bible in a setting which will appeal to hungering minds everywhere. It is in the light of this message that the deception of the immortal soul ideas, with all their related errors, will be seen for what they are. This will do much to prepare the way for the lightening of the world with glory of the Fourth Angel.

Another area in which the immortal soul idea has brought confusion and distortion is in the vital New Testament teaching of the second coming of Christ. This "blessed hope" (Titus 2:13) as it is known to many, has been virtually destroyed by the natural immortality teaching. Christ's second coming is tied in with such earth-shaking events as the resurrection of the righteous dead, the translation of the righteous living, and the related experience of the receiving of the heavenly rewards. But if man's reward has already been given him at death, then why the need for translation and resurrection? It is useless to argue that this will be a time for the reuniting of the "body" with the "soul," for how can this be regarded as some kind of reward, since immortal soul teachers generally look upon the body as the place where the soul is imprisoned and longs to be set free.[8] Surely a "soul" would feel bitter disappointment at having to be reunited with the body after enjoying years, perhaps eons, of ecstatic bliss! Inevitably, these ideas have made it impossible to keep alive the idea of a "blessed hope" of the soon return of Christ on the clouds of glory. All expressions of glad expectation, such as "near, even at the door," have lost their meaning in the fog of philosophies which teach of airy entities floating about in a spirit world of eternal bliss. If the righteous of all ages are already enjoying their reward and basking in the loveliness of Christ's eternal presence, then where is the excitement in hoping to meet Him on the clouds of glory at some time in the future? It is the imminence of Christ's return which fills His disciples with the gladness of joyful anticipation. The truth destroying doctrine of natural immortality has rendered all this meaningless.

7. Ellen G. White, *The Ellen G. White 1888 Materials*, The Ellen G. White Estate, Washington DC (1987), pp. 1336, 1337.

8. One book on the subject is entitled *Imprisoned Splendour* by Clarence Arthur Spaulding, Pioneer Press, Santa Ana, CA, 1966.

To reveal and demonstrate God's true character to the world, "His character of love," is the task of those who are to give the message of warning to this dying world.[9] How could this ever be done if, at the same time, He is to be portrayed as One who will torture sinners for every passing age of eternity? Again another of the deceptive tentacles of this immortal soul doctrine is revealed. As a means of destroying virtually all of the great central tenets of the Christian faith, the introduction of the idea of natural immortality has turned out to be a Satanic masterstroke! A more effective distortion of truth could hardly be devised. And it will be the task of those who fulfill the prophecy of the Fourth Angel, whose glory is to lighten the earth, to unmask every phase of this key deception and to sound the clarion call of truth to every corner of the globe with its hungering multitudes, and thus to prepare a people for the glorious return of our Lord.

---

9. Ellen G. White, *Christ's Object Lessons*, p. 415.

APPENDIX B

New Testament versus Roman Catholic Justification by Faith

(1) The Catholic view sees justification administered exclusively by the Catholic Church through its sacraments: "The instrumental cause is the sacrament of baptism." "The sacrament of Penance" is necessary to be administered by the same Church. Also "sacramental confession, ... sacerdotal absolution," "fasts, alms, prayers, and the other pious exercises" are needed.[1] In contrast, the New Testament teaches justification by faith in Christ alone, and the instrumentality is the Holy Spirit, not a church or hierarchy.

(2) The Catholic view denies that the sacrifice of Christ restored the whole race of men to favor with God. "Though He died for all, yet do not all receive the benefit of his death, but those only unto whom the merit of his passion is communicated" by the sacraments of the Church.[2] In contrast, the apostles' Good News says that *legally* "all ... [are] justified freely by his grace through the redemption that is in Christ Jesus"; "through one Man's righteous act the free gift came to all men, resulting in justification of life"; "He Himself is the propitiation for our sins, and not for ours only but also for the whole world"; "the Lamb of God ... takes away the sin of the world" (Romans 3:24; 5:18; 1 John 2:2; John 1:29)! "The judicial action, following upon the one offence [of Adam], issued in a verdict of condemnation, but the act of grace, following upon so many misdeeds, issued in a verdict of acquittal. ... The issue of one just act is acquittal and life for all men" (Romans 5:16, 18, NEB). Even Luther and Calvin were not able to see

---

1. Council of Trent, Sixth Session, Chapter VII; Chapter XIV. From Philip Schaff, *The Creeds of Christendom*, Vol. II, pp. 89-118.
2. Council of Trent, Chapter III.

clearly this larger New Testament vision of what Christ accomplished on His cross, effectively dying for the whole world.

(3) In Roman Catholic justification, the believer is not united to Christ through faith, by the free imputation of the whole of Christ's righteousness, but God gradually infuses his soul with an inherent righteousness that is meritorious, so that persevering Catholics will "have truly merited eternal life ... if so be, however, that they depart in grace."[3] The gospel message recognizes that the believer never has an iota of merit in himself, nor any righteousness inherent in himself; righteousness is only *in Christ* and the believer receives it only *by faith*. The Council of Trent can never truly provide assurance of justification. There is always the nagging "if" that carries over until the very moment of death.

(4) The Council of Trent taught that "adults ... may ... convert themselves to their own justification, by freely assenting to and co-operating with that said grace." This "anticipated ... grace of God" *precedes* justification and requires first a "disposition, or preparation, [which] is followed by Justification itself." The Trent Chapters VI and VII list many items of "preparation" that the sinner must do *before* he can be justified. These are "things which precede justification."[4] The gospel message recognizes that man has no part whatever in his justification and can make no preparation for it or do anything to "precede" it. It was done wholly by Christ, and all the believer can do is to receive, accept, believe, appreciate, the finished work of Christ, and stop hindering this dynamic faith to work obedience by love.

(5) The Catholic view encourages doubt and fear: "Each one, when he regards himself, and his own weakness and indisposition, may have fear and apprehension touching his own grace; seeing that no one can know with a certainty of faith, which can not be subject to error, that he has obtained the grace of God." "If any one saith, that it is necessary for every one, for the obtaining of remission of sins, that he believe for certain ... that his sins are forgiven him: let him be anathema."[5] The gospel message recognizes that "unto every one of us is given grace according to the measure of the gift of Christ," and encourages complete confidence in the gift of that grace (Ephesians 4:7).

---

3. Council of Trent, Chapter XVI.
4. Council of Trent, Chapter V; Chapter VII; Chapter VIII.
5. Council of Trent, Chapter IX; Canon XIII.

(6) The Catholic view fails to see that the whole fallen human race which is "in Adam" is corporately "in Christ" by virtue of His sacrifice. The gospel message sees sin as a continual, unbelieving resistance of Christ, who "will draw all men unto Me" if they will stop resisting. Christ has already tasted the second death "for everyone," and thus no one can suffer at last for his sins unless he disbelieves and rejects what Christ has done for him (John 12:32, KJV; Hebrews 2:9; John 3:17, 18).

(7) Thus the Catholic Church flatly denies that justification is by faith alone. When they say that justification "makes righteous," their idea is diametrically opposed to that of the gospel message. Catholic "justification" is infused, inherent, and meritorious, and not solely of faith: "No one ought to flatter himself up with faith alone, fancying that by faith alone he is made an heir, and will obtain the inheritance."[6]

The gospel breaks through centuries of Catholic and Protestant fog into a clearer view of the sunlit New Testament truth.

---

6. Council of Trent, Chapter XI.

Robert J. Wieland

1916-2011

As a boy, Robert J. Wieland read avidly and widely, and developed his growing writing talent. Listening to an old cracked Victrola recording of Jascha Heifetz started a lifetime of violin playing and a passion for classical music.

After graduating from the seminary at Emmanuel Missionary College near Washington, D.C., he became the pastor of a small church in St. Augustine, Florida. It was in Florida where he met Grace, which began 66 years of a devoted, loving, and supportive marriage that inspired and nurtured all those around them until Grace's death in 2008.

In 1945 they, and their young family of three, answered a call to become missionaries in Uganda, where Elder Wieland planted churches and a hospital that survived the Idi Amin regime. It was there that he discovered that in order to hold the people in the church the people needed to grasp the "most precious" truths of "Christ and Him crucified." This became the signature of his ministry and writings.

In 1952 the family moved to Nairobi, Kenya, where he was a pastor, church administrator, radio speaker, editor, and prolific writer. He was fluent in Luganda and Swahili, and many Africans still read his materials and remember him and Grace with love and appreciation.

After returning to the United States he pastored churches in California, and he and Grace retired there. But retirement was not in his "vocabulary" as he continued into his 90s to give seminars, and write articles and books. In order to share the Good News with a wider audience, he authored "Dial Daily Bread," an inspiring daily devotional message, the e-mail version of which is continuing into its 24th year. (To subscribe, write to dailybread@1888message.org.)

Publications by Robert J. Wieland

(A Partial List)

Books

Powerful Good News

In Search of the Cross: Learning to "Glory" in It

A New Look at God's Law: How the Ten Commandments Become Good News

The Gospel in Revelation (a verse-by-verse study)

The Gospel in Daniel (a verse-by-verse-study)

Ephesians—You've Been "Adopted": Paul's "Most Precious" Letter Verse-by-Verse

Mary Magdalene, The Woman the World Can Never Forget: The Bible Story

Gold Tried in the Fire: Re-discovering the Powerful Bible Idea of What Dynamic Faith Is

In Search of the Treasure of Faith

The Lion That Ran Away: Children's Stories From Africa ... and Other Places

Pamphlets and Other Publications

The Nearness of Your Savior

Taking the Deadlock Out of Wedlock

The Lady Who Said "Yes" to God

The Word That Turned the World Upside Down

The Backward Prayer

Islam Challenges the World

For more information concerning books and other materials authored by Robert J. Wieland, please contact CFI Book Division, P.O. Box 159, Gordonsville, Tennessee 38563.